ALABAM
FOOTBALL

ALABAMA'S FOOTBALL PRIDE

The 13 National Championships

RICHARD SIKES

Old Bay Publishing
Huntsville, Alabama

Library of Congress Cataloging-in-Publication data is available.
ISBN: 0-9745854-3-2; 978-09745854-3-7

Cover design by Hope Design
Cover photo: AP Images
Page design by Mike Towle

Printed in the United States of America
1 2 3 4 5 6—14 13 12 11 10

To the Angels, Megan and Paige

Contents

Acknowledgments

I WILL ALWAYS BE INDEBTED to retired *Huntsville Times* sports editor John Pruett who was so helpful with my first book, *Laughing With the Bear*, and whose amazingly accurate predictions about the 1992 team are quoted widely in Chapter 12. Tim Cohane's *Great College Football Coaches of the Twenties and Thirties* provided insights into coaches Wallace Wade and Frank Thomas. Dick Rockne's *Bow Down to Washington* and Fred Merrick's *Down on the Farm: Stanford Football* provided details on early Rose Bowl opponents. Background on Alabama football came from Winston Groom's *The Crimson Tide*, Chris Walsh's *Crimson Storm Surge*, Richard Scott's *Legends of Alabama Football*, and Coach Paul (Bear) Bryant's autobiography *Bear: The Hard Life and Good Times of Alabama's Coach Bryant*. The rolltide web site has a wealth of historical data. The staff of the Heritage Room at the Huntsville Public Library was always helpful as I dug through almost a hundred years of history in the pages of the *Huntsville Daily Times* and the *Huntsville Times*. Brad Green of the Paul W. Bryant Museum helped me find just the right pictures for the early days of Bama football, and Kevin O'Sullivan of AP Images provided photographs of this year's champions. Mike Towle is a great editor to work with, and he can always be counted upon to produce a high quality book. Judy Petty's cover design skills are unsurpassed. Besides moral support, my wife Nell did her usual fine editing and proofreading job.

Introduction

I BEGAN TO CLOSELY FOLLOW college football as I entered my teenage years in the early sixties. When Alabama won the national championship in 1961, I had the same feeling of pride that we were the absolute best at something that southerners must have experienced when the 1925 team beat Washington in the Rose Bowl. After getting "hooked" on Alabama football in 1961, I followed the Tide through the 1964-1965 national titles, and then suffered in the late sixties along with other Tide fans through the only lean times of Coach Paul "Bear" Bryant's tenure. The bad times were washed away when Coach Bryant implemented the wishbone offense and rang up three more national titles in the 1970's. Eight Southeastern Conference championships in the 1970's made Bama fans think that that was the natural order of the world.

Coach Bryant's retirement and death soon brought us Bammers back to reality; and after the Ray Perkins and Bill Curry eras, it seemed like the good times might never return. Then Gene Stallings had really good teams for most of his time in Tuscaloosa, topped off by dismantling Miami's upstart pretenders to the throne in the 1993 Sugar Bowl. After Coach Stallings retired to his Texas ranch, however, the program went downhill, with Mike DuBose losing control of the team in 2000. Although Dennis Franchione seemed to have the team on the right track, he was only at the Capstone briefly as a Texas-sized salary offer from Texas A&M and the handicap of NCAA penalties resulting from DuBose's tenure induced him to head to College Station. The program hit rock bottom when Mike Price's personal indiscretions led to his dismissal before he ever coached a game for the Crimson Tide. Mike Shula was hired under humiliating circumstances to replace the disgraced Price, and although Shula had one good year, Athletic Director Mal Moore correctly judged that Shula would never lead Bama back to its accustomed position among the college football elite.

As Nick Saban struggled to end a trying second season with the Miami Dolphins, Moore decided that Saban was the man who could restore the luster to the once proud Alabama football program. Moore relentlessly pursued the coach who had previously won a national title at LSU, and in early January 2007 Saban was introduced as the new coach in Tuscaloosa. When Saban was welcomed to Tuscaloosa with an unprecedented outpouring of enthusiasm, he came to realize the depth of Bama fans' affection for their Tide. Saban's first spring game in Tuscaloosa reinforced his feelings about the passion that Tide fans had for their team. Crowds of thirty thousand had been fairly common for the A-Day game that ended the spring practice program, but ninety-two thousand fans jammed into Bryant-Denny Stadium for Saban's first A-Day and thousands more were turned away.

As Saban took charge in Tuscaloosa, it became apparent to the new coach that his team was not entirely bereft of talent, but it was sorely lacking in work ethic and discipline. The new coach's "process" emphasized doing things right, not just winning football games. His goal was to remake the entire thought process of the Alabama football player, and not just come up with a game plan to win next Saturday's game. The "Saban process" emphasized doing everything you do well: academics and personal behavior as well as performance on the football field. The magnificent victory in Pasadena at the end of Saban's third year in Tuscaloosa confirmed for Alabama fans that their beloved football team had been restored to its rightful place atop the college football world.

- Richard Sikes
January 2010

I
1925:
The First Glorious Season

ALTHOUGH THE UNIVERSITY OF ALABAMA had fielded moderately successful football teams since 1892, compiling a record of 98-59-11, they had never received national recognition until they upset Coach John Heisman's University of Pennsylvania Quakers in 1922. Southern football at the time was considered to be inferior to that played in other parts of the country, and Alabama's 9-7 victory before twenty-five thousand fans in Philadelphia was a shock to the eastern football establishment.

University President George H. (Mike) Denny, an ardent supporter of the Alabama football program, had hired Coach Xen Scott in 1919 with instructions to build a strong football program that would enhance his plans to increase the enrollment and improve the prestige of the school. Scott accomplished his mission of putting Alabama football on the map as he compiled a 29-9-3 record in his four years in Tuscaloosa, but he resigned after the 1922 season, when he was diagnosed with terminal throat cancer.

At the time of Scott's resignation, Vanderbilt had one of the premier football programs in the South. Vandy's coach, Dan McGugin, was known as one of the most successful and innovative coaches in the country, and his assistant, Wallace Wade, was recognized as a young coach with great potential. Wade was considered a key element of the undefeated 1921 and 1922 Vanderbilt teams, and his reputation earned him an invitation to Lexington after the 1922 season to interview for the vacant head-coaching job with the University of Kentucky Wildcats. After Wade met with the UK selection committee, he was asked to wait in the lobby while the officials decided if he would be offered the job. When the committee took more time than Wade considered necessary to make their decision, the prospective coach burst into their conference room and chewed them out. As a parting shot, Wade told the UK committee that no matter where he coached, his teams would never lose to the Wildcats. Ironically, the committee had decided to hire Wade, but their tardiness in informing him of their decision cost Kentucky the opportunity to hire a coach who was destined for greatness.

After Wade's unsuccessful foray to Lexington, Alabama President Denny hired the Vandy assistant in 1923 to succeed Xen Scott to head the Crimson Tide program. Although Wade was a native of Trenton, Tennessee, he had learned his football while playing on the East Coast at Brown University. Wade, who had served as a cavalry captain in World War I, stressed discipline, repetitious practice sessions, and attention to detail. He built upon the foundation laid by Scott to produce a 7-2-1 record in his first season in Tuscaloosa. The 1924 team achieved an 8-1 record, with the only loss being to a powerful Centre College team. The last game of the 1924 season was a 33-0 victory over Georgia in front of twenty thousand fans in Birmingham. The victory over the Bulldogs gave the Crimson Tide their first Southern Conference championship, and it would be the first of many titles that Alabama brought to Tuscaloosa.

The 1924 conference championship season proved to be an apt precursor to the 1925 campaign. The 1925 squad, led by two All Americans in quarterback Allison (Pooley) Hubert and running back Johnny Mack Brown, was destined to bring Alabama football to the attention of the entire nation. Hubert was a fierce competitor and outstanding leader who had dropped out of high school to fight in World War I. The Meridian, Mississippi, native had been offered a football scholarship at Princeton after the war ended, but he arrived too late to take his entrance exams. Ultimately, he enrolled at Alabama as a twenty-one-year-old freshman in 1922. Hubert's teammates on the 1925 Alabama squad called the twenty-five-year-old senior "Papa Pooley." Hubert was a bruising running back and outstanding passer as well as being one of Bama's all-time greats as a defensive back. Halfback Johnny Mack Brown provided the speed to go with Hubert's brawn. The Dothan native's outstanding speed and open field running ability earned him the nickname "the Dothan Antelope."

Alabama opened the historic 1925 season with a 53-0 thrashing of Union College, and went on to score 277 points for the season while holding the opposition to seven points and winning their second straight Southern Conference title. Their only close games were a 7-0 victory over powerful Georgia Tech in Atlanta, and a 6-0 defeat of Mississippi State in Tuscaloosa. They thrashed Coach Wade's would-be Kentucky employers, 31-0, in Birmingham.

The Rose Bowl game, which had been played in Pasadena, California, on an annual basis since 1916, was the only football bowl game played in 1926. The classic in Pasadena had traditionally matched the

Pacific Coast champion with a powerhouse from the East or Midwest. Undefeated Washington had won the Pacific Coast Conference championship, and was the obvious choice to represent the West Coast. Dartmouth, Princeton, and Colgate were the class of the East, but they were not receptive to a trip to Pasadena since the American Association of University Professors had recently issued a report that was critical of football, saying the sport was thought to contribute to "drinking, dishonesty, and poor academics."

When the Tulane administration declined the invitation, the Rose Bowl finally turned to Tuscaloosa to find an opponent for Washington.

Although representatives of the Rose Bowl had been in Birmingham to observe Alabama's 27-0 rout of Georgia at the end of the season, they had not been impressed by the Crimson Tide's performance. Although Alabama had steamrolled their opposition in 1925, the brand of football played in the South was considered inferior, and a southern team had never been invited to play in Pasadena.

After being turned down by the eastern powers, however, the Rose Bowl officials decided to offer an invitation to Tulane, which had only a tie with Missouri marring its 1925 record, and Tulane had tied Alabama for the championship of the Southern Conference. When the Tulane administration declined the invitation, the Rose Bowl finally turned to Tuscaloosa to find an opponent for Washington. Although the University of Alabama had a rule prohibiting post-season play by the football team, Dr. Denny quickly rescinded the ban on bowl games and accepted the invitation to Pasadena.

After Alabama accepted the invitation to the bowl, most knowledgeable football fans gave the Crimson Tide little chance to defeat the mighty Huskies. Homespun philosopher-comedian Will Rogers reflected the mood of most fans when he observed that the University of Alabama was located in "Tusca-loser." Pigskin prognosticators expected the Crimson Tide to provide only modest opposition, and they predicted a Washington victory margin between fourteen and fifty points. Stanford Coach Pop Warner said that the southerners would not be able to stand up to the huge Washington line. Coach Wade thought that there was not much of a gap between the brand of football played in the South and the rest of the country, however, and he used the Crimson Tide's underdog status to motivate his team. The team traveled to Pasadena by train, and Wade conducted workouts at every stop along the way to the West Coast. He also brought along fifty-five-gallon drums of Alabama drinking water to insure against illness resulting from drinking "foreign" water. After their arrival in Pasadena, telegrams poured in from all over the South urging the Crimson Tide to fight for the honor of Dixie.

Alabama's opponent in the 1926 Rose Bowl game was one of the greatest teams ever fielded by Washington. The 1925 Huskies led the nation in scoring for the second time in three years. Coach Enoch Bagshaw's team was led by triple-threat halfback George (Wildcat) Wilson, halfback Elmer Tesreau, and quarterback George Guttormsen. The All-American Wilson was a hard-nosed running back with outstanding speed. He also was a fine passer, kicker, and a ferocious linebacker on defense in this era of one-platoon football. Tesreau was also an outstanding runner and stout defender, and Guttormsen was a fierce blocker, tough runner, and fine pass receiver.

As expected, Washington and Wildcat Wilson, who was described as "quick to start and hard to hold," dominated the game in the first half. A 55-yard drive in the first quarter culminated in a 1-yard touchdown run by Washington's Harold Patton. However, a wide PAT kick kept the Huskies' lead at 6-0. A 33-yard gallop by Wilson set up the second Husky touchdown, and his 20-yard pass to John Cole gave Washington their second score. Guttormsen's PAT kick hit the crossbar of the goalpost and bounced back to leave the Washington lead at 12-0. Just before halftime, however, Wilson made a play that forever changed the history of the state of Alabama. After Alabama's Johnny Mack Brown attempted to get to his feet after being tackled by the

Huskies' star, Wilson bent over and twisted the leg of the Alabamian. The "cheap shot" enraged the hitherto lethargic Crimson Tide, and shortly before the end of the first half they put a vicious hit on Wilson that knocked the Washington star unconscious. Wilson was forced out of the game, and he did not return until early in the fourth quarter. Shortly after Wilson was knocked out of the game, the Crimson Tide began a drive that reached the Husky 22, but the first half ended before they could score, and Washington went to halftime with a 12-0 lead.

At halftime an enraged Hubert reminded the Tide of Wilson's "cheap shot," and the Bama quarterback threatened retribution against his teammates if they didn't beat the Huskies. After the second half began, the teams exchanged punts, and Bama halfback Grant Gillis returned the Washington kick to the Husky 41. On Bama's first play, the fired-up Hubert ran 26 yards over left tackle. Then he blasted straight up the middle for 10 yards to put the ball on the Husky 5. Two more runs by the Tide quarterback put the ball on the Washington 2-yard line, and he scored the first Bama touchdown with a 2-yard run over center. Bill Buckler's PAT kick cut the Washington lead to 12-7. The crowd let out a tremendous roar as the underdogs from the South scored their first points.

Johnny Mack Brown, the "Dothan Antelope," scores his second touchdown against Washington in the third period of the 1926 Rose Bowl as an official looks on. Paul W. Bryant Museum.

After Alabama kicked off to Washington, the Crimson Tide defense held and forced a punt, which Johnny Mack Brown returned to the Bama 22. After several running plays advanced the ball to the Tide 35, halfback Grant Gillis hit Brown with a 65-yard TD pass. The crowd again roared as the underdog southerners took their first lead of the game, and Buckler's PAT kick increased Bama's lead to 14-12.

Washington fumbled on their first play after receiving Alabama's kickoff, and the Tide recovered the ball on the Husky 30. The Tide offense wasted no time in taking advantage of the turnover as Hubert tossed a TD pass to the Dothan Antelope on the first play after the fumble recovery. Buckler's wide PAT kick left the Tide lead at 20-12 as the third quarter ended. Bama's dramatic comeback had resulted in twenty points in slightly more than seven minutes. Although Johnny Mack Brown would later use his matinee idol looks to become the star of numerous Hollywood westerns, he never played a role that was as dramatic as the one played out on the stage of the Rose Bowl.

A huge cheer went up from the Washington fans as Wilson re-entered the game early in the final period, and the resurgent Huskies held the Tide on downs at the Washington 12. Wilson then led Washington on an 88-yard drive that ended with a 30-yard Wilson touchdown pass to Guttormsen. Gene Cooke's successful PAT kick cut the Bama lead to 20-19 with slightly over eight minutes left to play.

After Alabama returned the kickoff to their own 35, they proceeded to drive to the Washington 23 before Hubert threw an interception right into the arms of Washington end John Cole. However, Grant Gillis negated the impact of the Tide's turnover as he intercepted a Wilson pass, and returned it to the Bama 40. Alabama was unable to pick up a first down, but

Wilson's last-second desperation pass was intercepted by Herschel Caldwell as the game ended.

Caldwell's interception set off a jubilant celebration among the Tide supporters in the massive stadium, and the fans of the mighty Huskies sat in stunned silence. Walter Eckersall, a highly respected sportswriter for the *Chicago Tribune* who had also officiated the game, wrote that the Alabama victory had "placed the southern brand of football on a par at least with that played in other sections of the country." The Rose Bowl victory over the Pacific Coast Conference champions catapulted Alabama to the top of the college football world, and they were generally considered to be the best football team in the country that year. After their Rose Bowl victory, Alabama was no longer considered only a regional football power, they were considered worthy of national attention.

There were no national radio networks in 1926, and southern fans gathered in theaters and auditoriums to follow the game as results were called out from tickertape transmissions. As soon as news of the Rose Bowl victory reached the South, wild celebrations erupted throughout the region. Unlike the northern states, the economy of the South had never recovered from the devastation of the Civil War, and the region had developed an inferiority complex. While the North had experienced rapid industrial growth after the war ended, the South remained a largely rural society. Northerners considered the area below the Mason-Dixon Line to be the land of illiterate, hookworm-infested sharecroppers. The Alabama football team had come to represent not only their own state, but the entire southern region in their showdown with the "yankees" from the University of Washington.

The victory of the Crimson Tide brought pride to southerners who had paid little attention to the game of football before January 1, 1926. It united the entire region more than any event since the Civil War had ended some sixty years earlier. Southern newspapers hailed the Crimson Tide's victory in Pasadena as the South's greatest victory since Robert E. Lee's surrender at Appomattox. Thousands participated in a spontaneous parade honoring the team in Montgomery. Celebrations led by University of Alabama students and alumni broke out around the state. Brass bands met the conquering heroes in nearly every southern town as the train brought the Crimson Tide back to Tuscaloosa. A huge throng, including many Tulane students, met the train in New Orleans.

Tuscaloosa had a wild victory celebration that newspaper reports said, "painted the city red from the Warrior River to the furthest confines of the town." The newspaper also reported that "after the game ended, unrestrained joy reigned in the seat of the university as plans were immediately begun for a reception unlike any ever given to a football team in the South." Tuscaloosa officials saluted the football team for making "both the University and the state famous overnight."

When the team completed its triumphant return home on January 5, the victorious warriors were met by a huge crowd and loaded on large, decorated wagons that were pulled by freshmen students along the parade route. After they were welcomed home by the president of the alumni association, Governor W. W. Brandon welcomed them back to the state on behalf of two and a half million Alabamians, and assured them that they had "written history for Alabama which will never be forgotten."

2
1926:
Back to Pasadena

THE FOOTBALL COACHING PROFESSION has always been one with a heavy emphasis on what have you done for me lately, and Wallace Wade found that to be the case as he prepared his team for the 1926 season. All Americans Johnny Mack Brown and Pooley Hubert were seniors when they had led the Crimson Tide to their improbable Rose Bowl triumph to end the 1925 campaign, and Wade would have to find replacements for his two biggest stars in the new year. Despite the loss of Brown and Hubert, the 1926 team was not completely bereft of talent, as fifteen of the twenty-three players on the 1925 national championship team returned to play the following season. Wade was optimistic as he approached the new season as he explained that he had nine returning lettermen—four of whom were starters on the 1925 squad.

Although the 1926 team was not as dominant as the previous squad, they outscored their opponents 242-20 in the regular season. The cornerstones of the team were All-American end Hoyt (Wu) Winslett and All-Conference tackle Freddie Pickhard, both of whom had played on the Tide's first Rose Bowl team the previous year. Although Winslett played as an end, he was frequently utilized as a runner and passer in Wade's offense.

The first major test for the 1926 team was a matchup with Coach Wade's mentor Dan McGugin and his Vanderbilt Commodores in Nashville. The Crimson Tide passed their first major test as halfback Red Barnes scored two rushing touchdowns, and Winslett threw a 9-yard touchdown pass to Herschel Caldwell for another score as the Crimson Tide prevailed, 19-7, over the Commodores. The victory over Vanderbilt was followed by a 26-7 win over Mississippi State (then called Mississippi A&M). Next came a 21-0 victory over Georgia Tech in Atlanta that was the worst defeat that the Yellow Jackets had absorbed in eleven years. Georgia Tech's student newspaper, *The Technique*, said that Winslett was one of the "prettiest passers that has chunked a football in Grant Field." The Tide All American completed only 4 of 10 attempts,

After three games against teams that were considered stout opposition, the Crimson Tide looked forward to a relative breather against the Sewanee Tigers.

but three of the passes were for touchdowns. *The Technique* described the "crimson jersied lads" as one of the best teams that Atlanta fans had seen in some time. The newspaper also said that the 1926 edition of the Crimson Tide was superior to the 1925 Rose Bowl champions, and that, in comparison to Georgia Tech, the Alabama players were heavier "and no doubt smarter" than the Yellow Jackets.

After three games against teams that were considered stout opposition, the Crimson Tide looked forward to a relative breather against the Sewanee Tigers. The Sewanee contest was the first played in Birmingham since the victory in Pasadena, and fans eagerly snapped up tickets to watch the Tide, who were two-touchdown favorites to beat the Tigers. Although Sewanee came into the game with a modest 2-1 record, they had three things working in their favor: a line that averaged two hundred pounds, including a massive (for that day) 260-pound center; an extra week of practice to get ready for Alabama; and a strong desire to make a name for themselves by knocking off one of the top teams in the country.

Bama struggled throughout the Sewanee game and did not seem to be the same team that had scored impressive wins over Vanderbilt, Mississippi State, and Georgia

Tech. The Tigers outplayed the Crimson Tide for most of the scoreless game, but with only a minute to play Alabama blocked a punt on the Sewanee 9-yard line and the ball bounced out of the end zone for a safety to give the Tide a 2-0 victory. Although the underdog Tigers had lost, their fans, in a prelude to the thought process for Bama opponents in the next eighty-plus years, considered the close score to be a "moral victory."

After the squeaker over Sewanee, the Tide posted victories over LSU, Kentucky, Florida, and Georgia, a four-game stretch in which they outscored the opposition 120-6 with only Georgia scoring any points in a 33-6 loss in Birmingham. The undefeated Crimson Tide, who had won twenty straight games by the end of the 1926 season, earned their third consecutive Southern Conference title that year, and they were invited back to Pasadena to defend their Rose Bowl title against the undefeated Stanford Cardinal. (Until 1930, Stanford didn't actually have a mascot and "Cardinal" was used as a generic reference. They became the Indians in 1930, only to officially revert back to the Cardinal in 1981.)

Although Stanford had not been as dominant as Alabama in the 1926 campaign, they had won all of their games and were champions of the Pacific Coast Conference. The Cardinal were also awarded the Rissman National Trophy, which was given to the top team in the country at the conclusion of the regular season. The Pacific champions were led by three All Americans: end Ted Shipkey, guard Fred Swan, and halfback George Bogue. Additionally, "Tricky" Dick Hyland was an outstanding halfback.

Since the Rose Bowl invitations to Alabama and Stanford had been issued earlier than usual, Stanford's coach, the legendary Glenn (Pop) Warner, had a chance to scout the Crimson Tide before their arrival on the West Coast. Warner had been impressed by the speed of the southerners, and he ordered silk pants for his team to wear to increase their speed. Unlike the heavily favored Washington team that had been surprised by Alabama in the 1926 Rose Bowl, Pop Warner was determined not to be surprised by the visitors from the southland.

A crowd of 57,417, the largest in Rose Bowl history until that time, saw Stanford complete a 38-yard pass to Hyland on the first play of the game, but that drive bogged down at the Bama 18, and Bogue's field goal attempt was wide. Another Cardinal threat was stopped by a fumble, but on its third possession Stanford drove 63 yards for a touchdown with George Bogue hitting end Ed Walker with a 20-yard pass for the score. A successful PAT conversion gave the Cardinal a 7-0 lead late in the first quarter.

Stanford was unable to score again, although they dominated the rest of the game. Despite Stanford's ability to move the ball, the hard-nosed Crimson Tide defense rose to the occasion when it looked like the westerners were about to put more points on the scoreboard. Finally, with about four minutes to play, Bama's Clarke (Babe) Pearce leaped high to block a Stanford punt, and the Crimson Tide recovered the ball on the Cardinal 14. After the Tide took possession, it took them only four plays to score as halfback Jimmy Johnson, who had missed most of the game with a dislocated shoulder, went over right guard into the end zone to cut the Stanford lead to 7-6. Stanford was determined to block Herschel Caldwell's PAT kick, but a trick play allowed Bama to snap the ball before the Cardinal defense was set, and the successful kick tied the game at 7-7. Stanford was able to run only three plays after receiving the Tide kickoff, and the game ended in a 7-7 tie.

The stunned crowd could not believe the final score. They could not comprehend how a team that had been as thoroughly outplayed as the Tide had not lost the game. Bama had gained only 98 yards of offense to their opponents' 305. The Crimson Tide had completed only 1 of 7 pass attempts for 9 yards, while the Cardinal hit 12 of 16 for 175 yards. Although the West

Coast fans were astounded that their team had not won, they were impressed by the gritty southerners' ability to do what was necessary to avert defeat. Since the Crimson Tide had tied the national champion Cardinal, they were recognized as co-champions by the Helms Athletic Foundation.

With well-known sportscaster Graham McNamee providing the play-by-play commentary on the NBC radio network, the 1927 Rose Bowl game was the first to be broadcast coast-to-coast. Judge James J. Mayfield, a former justice of the Alabama Supreme Court, had a heart attack and died while listening to the radio broadcast. Friends who were listening to the game with the judge said his last words were "Why don't they resort to the pass?" The *Huntsville Daily Times* set up a radio outside their building to allow Huntsvillians to listen to the game. The paper reported that the crowd's spirits were "almost deflated" throughout most of the game as Stanford led 7-0, but when Bama scored to tie the game "most of the gang went stark crazy, dancing around as if they were with the Alabama rooters in the Far West."

3

1930:
Wallace Wade's Grand Finale

AFTER COMPILING A RECORD of 19-0-1 in 1925/1926 that included two trips to the Rose Bowl, Alabama's performance slipped somewhat in the next three years. The 1927 team had a rebuilding year and could manage only a 5-4-1 record, and the 6-3 records in both 1928 and 1929 were only slightly better. Although these records would have been welcomed at many schools, Alabama fans and alumni grumbled that coach Wallace Wade seemed to have lost his touch.

Wade had never had a good relationship with President Denny, whom he thought meddled too much in team affairs, and the coach took the fans' complaints about the increasing number of losses personally. His success at Alabama had caught the attention of football fans and college athletic officials around the country, and prior to the 1930 season he was approached by Duke University officials about coaching the Blue Devils. After being offered a fairly large increase in salary and given assurances that he would have more control over the football program, Wade signed a contract to coach the Blue Devils beginning in 1931. Since he had one year remaining on his contract with Alabama, his tenure at Duke would not begin until after the 1930 season.

As Coach Wade negotiated his contract with Duke, he knew that his last Alabama team would be an outstanding group, but even he probably did not realize how strong the team would be. The 1930 squad included four All Americans: tackles Fred Sington and C. B. (Foots) Clement and halfbacks John (Flash) Suther and Johnny (Sugar) Cain. Other stars included quarterback John (Monk) Campbell, guards Frank Howard (the future Clemson coach) and John Miller, center Jess Eberdt, and receiver Jimmy Moore. The Tide was so talented and had so much depth that Coach Wade let the second string start the games, and he did not put the first team in the game until the second quarter.

The season began with easy victories over Howard College, Mississippi, and Sewanee in which the Tide outscored their opponents 132-0. Then came the first big test of the 1930 season: a showdown with Tennessee in Tuscaloosa. Tennessee had beaten the Tide 15-13 in 1928 and 6-0 in 1929, and Coach Wade had never defeated Robert Neyland, the up-and-coming coach of the Volunteers. Alabama stopped their losing streak to Neyland in 1930, however, with an 18-6 victory over the Big Orange and their outstanding quarterback Bobby Dodd. They followed the victory over Tennessee with a 12-7 squeaker over Vanderbilt in Birmingham. The Crimson Tide then ended the season with double-digit shutout victories over Kentucky, Florida, LSU, and Georgia in which Bama scored eighty-five points. The 1930 Southern Conference championship was the fourth won by Wade's teams in his eight years in Tuscaloosa.

Tennessee had beaten the Tide 15-13 in 1928 and 6-0 in 1929, and Coach Wade had never defeated Robert Neyland, the up-and-coming coach of the Volunteers.

After their strong showing in 1930, Alabama was invited back to Pasadena, this time to face Washington State College in the Rose Bowl. Coach Babe Hollingbery's Cougars, also undefeated, had won the championship of the Pacific Coast Conference. Before the game the Cougars' coach was upbeat about his team's chances. Although Hollingbery conceded that Alabama had the best team in its history and possibly the best in the history of the South, he thought his team had a chance to beat the Crimson Tide.

In keeping with his usual pattern, Coach Wade started the bowl game with the second-stringers on the field, and they were able to keep Washington State from scoring in the first quarter. When the first string entered the game in the second period, it was not long before Flash Suther got behind the Cougars' secondary and grabbed a 62-yard pass from Jimmy Moore for the first score of the game. Monk Campbell's PAT kick gave the Tide a 7-0 lead.

Shortly thereafter, center Jess Eberdt intercepted a Washington State pass on the Cougars' 31. Then end Ben Smith outjumped two Cougar defenders to grab a 30-yard pass from Moore to move the ball to the WSC 1. Campbell then scored on a 1-yard run, and kicked the PAT to make it 14-0 for Bama.

On Bama's next possession, Campbell ran 43 yards off right tackle for his second touchdown of the game to increase the lead to 21-0 before halftime. The Tide had scored 21 points in six minutes, and Washington State would never be in the game after the second-quarter surge. In the third quarter J. B. (Ears) Whitworth kicked a 40-yard field goal for the last score of the game. After the last Bama score, the Cougars unleashed an all-out passing barrage to attempt to get back into the game. Washington State did advance to the 2-yard line of the Tide, but Fred Sington recovered a fumble to thwart the Cougars' best scoring opportunity of the game.

Alabama dominated the final statistics as much as they dominated the scoreboard. The Tide's balanced offense gained 396 yards while holding the Cougars to 261. In addition, the Tide defense completely throttled the Cougars' offense with three pass interceptions and three fumble recoveries. Associated Press sportswriter Paul D. Zimmerman said that Alabama was superior in "brains, brawn, and deception." Cougars Coach Hollingbery said, "The defeat was a big surprise to me," but Wallace tersely replied that he could think of "no comment to make" after the game.

Alabama was voted the 1930 national champion in several polls, and when Wallace Wade left Tuscaloosa he had won three national titles in his last six years. However, he left with hard feelings toward President Denny, and when he was presented a silver tray at his final football awards banquet with the Crimson Tide, Wade only said, "There are many things you might like to hear me say, but I cannot say them. There are many things I might like to say, but I cannot, so I'll just sit down." To make sure that his message was understood, he left the silver tray that had been presented to him on the podium.

Although his departure was tinged with bitterness, Wallace Wade is a revered figure to Crimson Tide fans. In eight seasons he had won the championship of the Southern Conference four times in addition to his three national titles, and he had moved Alabama into the elite schools of college football. When the 1930 team had a fifty-year reunion in 1980, coach Paul (Bear) Bryant introduced Wallace Wade to his team by saying "Men, I'd like you to meet Coach Wallace Wade, the man who is most responsible for the University of Alabama football tradition. In many ways, he is the reason I'm here and the reason you're here."

4

1934:

Coach Thomas's First Title

AFTER WALLACE WADE TOLD University of Alabama President George Denny that he would be leaving Alabama for Duke after the 1930 season, the coach recommended that Frank Thomas replace him as coach of the Crimson Tide. Thomas, a native of Muncie, Indiana, had grown up in East Chicago, Indiana, and had been the quarterback on Knute Rockne's 1922 Notre Dame team. His roommate at Notre Dame had been the legendary George Gipp, and the future Bama coach and his legendary roommate would frequently discuss football all hours of the night.

After Thomas earned a law degree from Notre Dame, he was hired to be an assistant coach at Georgia in 1923. After two years with the Bulldogs, Thomas took the head coaching job with the University of Chattanooga. He had an outstanding 26-9-2 record in his four years at Chattanooga, but was persuaded that a return to Georgia as an assistant would put him on a faster track to a better head coaching job.

In Coach Wade's resignation letter to University of Alabama president Dr. Denny, the departing coach had told the president that Thomas had played for Rockne and said, "Rock called him one of the smartest players he ever coached. I don't believe you could pick a better man."

Although Dr. Denny had great respect for Wade's football knowledge, he wanted to meet Coach Thomas before finalizing a job offer, so the president set up a meeting with the prospective coach and some Alabama boosters in Birmingham. After Thomas had signed his contract to coach the Crimson Tide, the university president told the newly hired coach: "Mr. Thomas, now that you have accepted our proposition, I will give you the benefit of my views based on many years of observation. It is my conviction that material is 90 percent and coaching is 10 percent. I desire further to say that you will be provided with the 90 percent, and that you will be held to strict accounting for delivering the remaining 10 percent."

After Thomas and a colleague had left the meeting, the newly hired coach said, "Those were the hardest and coldest words that I have ever heard in my entire life. Do you reckon those 90 and 10 percent figures are right?" Thomas's colleague said, "I think the figures are considerably off, but there is no doubt that the good doctor means what he says."

As the 1931 season approached, few football experts were optimistic about the prospects for the new Alabama coach. The Crimson Tide had only one starter returning from the 1930 juggernaut. In addition to the turnover in personnel, the installation of Thomas's Notre Dame offense was also projected to hinder the Tide's performance. However, the new Bama coach confounded the experts as his first team posted a 9-1 record. The only loss was a 25-0 setback at the hands of Robert Neyland's Tennessee Vols, and the only close victories were 9-7 over Kentucky and 14-6 over Vanderbilt. The Crimson Tide outscored the opposition 360-51.

The 1932 record was almost as good with only a 7-3 setback to Tennessee and a 6-0 shutout loss to Georgia Tech in Atlanta spoiling the year. The 1933 team then finished 7-1-1 as Coach Thomas finally beat Tennessee, but lost to Fordham (2-0 in New York City) and played Ole Miss to a scoreless tie in Birmingham. The 12-6 victory over Tennessee enabled Bama to win the first championship in the newly created Southeastern Conference.

Coach Thomas's 1931 recruiting class would prove to be one of the best ever brought to the Capstone, and when they were seniors in 1934, they formed the nucleus of one of Alabama's best teams of all time. On a squad loaded with stars, none shone brighter than triple-threat quarterback Millard (Dixie) Howell of tiny Hartford, Alabama. He was an outstanding open-field runner as well as a strong inside runner, a good punter, and an amazingly accurate passer. Howell still holds the Alabama record for the longest punt with an 89-yarder against Tennessee in 1933; he also booted an 83-yarder versus Kentucky that year.

Although Bryant was no match for the All-American Hutson as a pass receiver, he was an adequate receiver and a hard-nosed blocker and defender.

Coach Thomas said that end Don Hutson, who was on the receiving end of many of Howell's passes, was the greatest player he ever saw. The native of Pine Bluff, Arkansas, ran the 100-yard dash in 9.8 seconds, and his long effortless stride frequently fooled defensive backs into thinking he was not running very fast. He also ran precise pass patterns and had outstanding hands. The team's other end, Paul (Bear) Bryant, also hailed from Arkansas, and although Bryant was no match for the All-American Hutson as a pass receiver, he was an adequate receiver and a hard-nosed blocker and defender.

The two Alabama ends would have an impact far beyond the 1934 season. Hutson would help revolutionize the passing game in professional football with the Green Bay Packers, and thus greatly improve the popularity of the sport at the professional level. Bryant would become a legendary coach who would rank as the all-time winningest coach at the time of his retirement from Alabama in 1982. In addition to Howell and Hutson, center and team captain Bill Lee was also an All American. Riley Smith, another outstanding back on the 1934 team and a ferocious blocker, would make the All-American team in 1935. Jim Angelich was also an outstanding running back; Charlie Marr was a ferocious tackler from his guard position; and Joe Demyanovich was an outstanding fullback.

The football experts had predicted that Alabama in 1934 would be a strong contender in the Southeastern Conference and possibly nationally, and the Tide quickly validated those opinions as they opened the season with three victories over lightweight opponents Howard, Sewanee, and Mississippi State by a combined score of 100-6. After the three easy wins, the undefeated Tennessee Volunteers arrived for the annual showdown in Birmingham. Since both teams had outstanding teams every year, the UT-Bama showdown usually had national implications as well, giving the winner a leg up in the race for the championship of the Southeastern Conference.

Two famous ends from Arkansas from 1934 championship team: All-American pass receiver Don Hutson (right) and the "other end" and future coaching legend, Paul (Bear) Bryant. Paul W. Bryant Museum.

As was usually the case in matchups between Frank Thomas and Robert Neyland, the 1934 game was a low-scoring, hard-fought classic. After a scoreless first quarter, a 33-yard pass from Howell to Hutson set up the first Bama touchdown, which came on a Demyanovich run over left guard. The PAT was missed and the Tide lead was 6-0. Later in the second quarter, Alabama was penalized for "slugging" with Paul Bryant mistakenly identified as "the slugger." Although Bryant and his teammates loudly protested that the Bear was nowhere near where the infraction occurred, the future coaching legend was removed from the game. After Bryant was ejected, Tennessee fought back and was able to tie the score before the end of the first half, although the Volunteers also missed their PAT.

Howell's punting gave Alabama an advantage in field position in the third period and at one point allowed the Tide to get the ball on the UT 22-yard line. The Tide did not squander the good field position, and they picked up 6 yards on an end-around run by Hutson, 9 yards on a Howell-to-Hutson pass, and then Hutson slashed into the end zone on a 7-yard run. Riley Smith's successful PAT kick gave Bama a 13-6 lead.

Tennessee threatened to score twice, but the stout Bama defense rose to the occasion each time. Once, Tennessee's punt returner seemed to be headed for a touchdown until an outstanding tackle by Howell saved the day. On another occasion an outstanding play by center Kay Francis allowed the Tide to stop Tennessee on downs deep in Tide territory. Howell's performance running, passing, and punting led Coach Neyland to proclaim him the best back in the South.

The victory over Tennessee was followed by twenty-point wins over both Georgia and Kentucky and consecutive 40-0 blowouts of Clemson and Georgia Tech. The final game of the season was against Vanderbilt in Birmingham. Before the game Coach Thomas called the starting eleven together in the locker room, where he read a telegram from an official in the Stanford University athletic department that said a decisive Alabama victory would insure an invitation to play Stanford in the 1935 Rose Bowl. After the Rose Bowl incentive was added, the Commodores did not stand a chance, and they were annihilated 34-0. In his autobiography Coach Bryant said that he could hear the Million Dollar Band playing "California, Here I Come" as the starters were taken out of the game in the fourth quarter.

After the train trip to the West Coast, the team was ensconced in the Huntington Hotel where all the movie stars congregated. The team met Dick Powell and Mickey Rooney, and the young Paul Bryant had his picture made with starlet Lana Turner. Legendary sportswriters Grantland Rice and Braven Dyer were also there to cover the game.

The 1934 Stanford team was nicknamed the "Vow Boys" because as freshmen they had vowed never to lose to Southern California. They were talented enough to make the vow good as they beat USC all three years and went to the Rose Bowl in 1934, 1935, and 1936. The 1934 Stanford team had only a 7-7 tie with Santa Clara to blemish their record, and they had allowed opponents to score only two touchdowns. Coach Tiny Thornhill's Indians were led by Bobby Grayson, who was one of their all-time great running backs. Other stars included running back Robert (Bones) Hamilton, end Monk Moscrip, and tackle Robert (Horse) Reynolds. Bryant said that he had nightmares about having to go up against the monstrous All-American Reynolds. After Hutson met Reynolds at a media event a few days before the game, he put Bryant's mind at ease by telling him he had no reason to worry about the Stanford tackle, whom Hutson described as looking like Ichabod Crane. When Bryant finally saw Reynolds on the field before the game he knew that Hutson had been pulling his leg; Reynolds was a massive six-foot-four and weighed about 250, or about fifty pounds more than Bryant.

When Bryant finally saw Reynolds on the field before the game he knew that Hutson had been pulling his leg.

Many Stanford boosters had wanted the Indians to play Minnesota that year, because they thought a win over the undefeated Golden Gophers would be more prestigious than a victory over the Crimson Tide. Early in the first quarter Stanford recovered an Alabama fumble on the Tide 29, and shortly thereafter Grayson scored on a one-foot plunge to give the Indians a 7-0 lead.

After Grayson gave Stanford the early lead, the Stanford partisans in the crowd of eighty-five thousand began to chant, "We Want Minnesota." The "We Want Minnesota" chant immediately fired up the Crimson Tide. Will Rogers said that it was "like holding up a picture of Sherman's march to the sea in front of them Alabama boys." Although the Tide offense had gained only 4 yards on four plays in the entire first quarter, the fired-up southerners went to work quickly after Stanford took the lead. Howell began the offensive with a 25-yard punt return. Then Dixie completed a pass to the Indians' 5-yard line, and on the next play he ran it into the end zone to cut the lead to 7-6 (the PAT failed).

In those days the scored-upon team could elect to receive or kick off, and Stanford foolishly elected to kick off to Alabama. After the kickoff went out of the end zone, Bama took over on the 20-yard line and Howell's passes soon had them on the Stanford 5. Although Stanford's defense held, Riley Smith kicked a 22-yard field goal to give the Tide a 9-7 lead that caused the "We Want Minnesota" chants from the Stanford fans to die down considerably. Stanford again kicked off, and Howell returned the kick to the Tide 25. After Bama advanced the ball to their 33, Howell utilized outstanding blocks by practically the entire team to scamper 67 yards for his second TD of the game. Smith's PAT kick increased the Crimson Tide lead to 16-7.

Stanford belatedly decided it was better to receive than to give, and after Howell's second score Bama kicked off to the Indians. Shortly thereafter, the Tide picked off a Stanford pass at the Bama 46. Joe Riley, who had replaced Howell when Dixie developed stomach cramps, then tossed a 54-yard bomb to Hutson for another TD with only eight seconds left in the first half. Another missed PAT left the halftime Bama lead at 22-7.

Stanford scored a meaningless touchdown in the third quarter to cut the Bama lead to 22-13, but the Howell-to-Hutson combination clicked in the final period for a 59-yard scoring pass to close out the scoring at 29-13. With Alabama well ahead in the fourth quarter, Crimson Tide fans began to chant, "We Want Minnesota." After the Rose Bowl victory, Alabama was designated as 1934 national champions by several authorities including the Football Thesaurus, the Dunkel Index, and the Houlgate System.

By the time Dixie Howell had left the game in the fourth quarter, he had rushed for 111 yards, completed 9 of 12 pass attempts for 160 yards, and punted six times for a 43.8 yard average. After the game Coach Thomas compared Howell to his old Notre Dame roommate, George Gipp. Famed sportswriter Grantland Rice wrote, "Dixie Howell, the human howitzer from Hartford, Alabama, blasted the Rose Bowl dreams of Stanford with one of the greatest all-around exhibitions that football has ever seen." Will Rogers wisecracked, "If people in Arizona, Texas, or Arkansas hear something whizzing over their heads, it won't be a plane. It's Dixie Howell passing some autographed footballs back to friends in Tuscaloosa." Ralph McGill wrote in the *Atlanta Constitution* that "no team in the history of football, anywhere, anytime, has passed the ball as Alabama passed it today. And no man ever passed as did Dixie Howell, the swift sword of the Crimson attack."

5

1941:

Amidst the Clouds of War

After the 1934 team's decisive victory over Stanford in the Rose Bowl, the next six years produced some outstanding teams but no national championships. Dixie Howell, Bill Lee, and Don Hutson finished their careers in the 1935 Rose Bowl, and the 1935 Crimson Tide finished 6-3-1 as Coach Thomas completed a major rebuilding job. Riley Smith earned All-American honors as a quarterback in 1935, but the most memorable event of the year was Paul Bryant's performance in a 25-0 win over Tennessee. The senior end had broken the fibula in his right leg in a 20-7 loss to Mississippi State (Bama's first loss in Denny Stadium) on the Saturday prior to the UT game, and he had hobbled around on crutches the following week as the Tide prepared to play UT in Knoxville. Although Bryant had no intention of playing against the Vols, he quickly changed his mind when assistant coach Hank Crisp opened his pre-game pep talk by saying, "I don't know about the rest of you, but I know one damn thing, old 34 (Bryant's number) will be after them, he'll be after their butts." The young end was so inspired by Coach Hank's oratory that not only did he play, but he played the best game of his career.

After the relatively poor record in 1935, the 1936 team was undefeated with only a scoreless tie with Tennessee marring an otherwise perfect season. The tie with the Volunteers cost the 1936 team a bowl invitation, but the 1937 team's perfect 9-0 regular season and SEC championship earned them another trip to the Rose Bowl. However, the 1937 team's 13-0 loss to California, which would be the Crimson Tide's only loss in the Pasadena bowl, ended any hopes of a national title. The 1938 season opened with a 19-7 victory over Southern California in Los Angeles; the only blemishes on that year's record were a 13-0 loss to Tennessee and a 14-14 tie with Georgia Tech. Although the 1939 team would compile only a 5-3-1 record, the five wins included a 7-6 triumph over national power Fordham whose fierce line, nicknamed "the Seven Blocks of Granite," was led by

Vince Lombardi. The record in 1940 improved to 7-2, with the losses being to Mississippi State and a third straight loss to Tennessee.

The season got off to an inauspicious start as blocked kicks, intercepted passes and lost fumbles proved to be disastrous in a 14-0 shutout loss to Mississippi State in the second game of the year.

The 1941 team was loaded with talent, with halfback Jimmy Nelson, end Holt Rast, center Joe Domnanovich, and tackle Don Whitmire leading the way. However, the season got off to an inauspicious start as blocked kicks, intercepted passes and lost fumbles proved to be disastrous in a 14-0 shutout loss to Mississippi State in the second game of the year. After a blowout 61-0 victory over Howard College, halfback Jimmy Nelson's running, passing, punting, and three interceptions were key elements in a hard-fought 9-2 victory over Tennessee that snapped a three-game losing streak against the Volunteers.

After the Tennessee game, Bama defeated Georgia, 27-14, in a showdown between Jimmy Nelson and Georgia's outstanding triple-threat back (and 1942 Heisman Trophy winner) Frank Sinkwich. After wins over Kentucky, Tulane, and Georgia Tech, the Crimson Tide was upset 7-0 by Vanderbilt. The Vandy defense completely shut down the Alabama offense in a game played in ankle-deep mud during a driving rainstorm in

Nashville. However, the Tide bounced back from the upset loss to the Commodores to close out the regular season with a 21-7 victory over Miami.

After the victory over Miami, Alabama accepted its first-ever bid to a bowl game other than the Rose Bowl when they accepted an invitation to face Texas A&M's aerial circus in the Cotton Bowl. Coach Homer Norton's Aggies had the best passing attack in the country, which is why Coach Thomas worked long and hard on pass defense in preparing for the Aggies. Since A&M had gained 1,658 passing yards during the regular season and Alabama's rushing attack had gained 1,698 yards, the Cotton Bowl figured to be a shootout between two different offensive styles. However, the weather on New Year's Day in Dallas was horrible, and Alabama's work on pass defense was the key to stopping A&M on a muddy field. Although the Aggies outgained the Crimson Tide by 194 yards to 16 through the air, Alabama intercepted seven A&M passes and recovered five fumbles as they romped to a 29-21 victory.

Although A&M had thirteen first downs to only one for the Tide, and outgained the Tide 309-75 in total yards, Bama utilized the twelve Aggie turnovers and a 72-yard Jimmy Nelson punt return for a touchdown to build a 29-7 lead midway through the fourth quarter. Two fourth-quarter A&M touchdowns against Bama reserves gave the bizarre game the appearance of being closer than it actually was.

Although Minnesota was proclaimed national champions by most rating systems, Texas and Alabama were declared co-champions by the Houlgate system that used mathematical formulas to evaluate teams from 1927-58. The Houlgate system was actually the first systematic approach to determining a national champion in college football.

The 1942 bowl games were overshadowed by World War II, which had begun more than three weeks earlier and would fundamentally affect college football and all other aspects of American life for the next four years.

6
1961:
Return to Glory

ALTHOUGH COACH FRANK THOMAS never won another national championship after 1941, his next four teams had respectable records, and the 1945 team, which had a perfect 10-0 mark, won the SEC championship. The 1942 team made Bama's first trip to the Orange Bowl; the 1944 season ended with their first trip to the Sugar Bowl; and the 1945 season finale ended with a 34-14 triumph over Southern Cal in Bama's last appearance in the Rose Bowl. However, high blood pressure and heart problems led to Thomas's retirement after the 1946 season. Harold (Red) Drew, who had served as an assistant to Coach Thomas, returned from a one-year stint as head coach at Ole Miss to succeed his former boss as head coach in Tuscaloosa in 1947. Although Drew's teams were good enough to go to the Sugar Bowl in 1948, the Orange Bowl in 1953 (a 61-6 victory over Syracuse), and the 1954 Cotton Bowl, his total record in Tuscaloosa was *only* 54-28-7, and his 4-5-2 record in 1954 led to his ouster.

Drew's successor, J. B. (Ears) Whitworth presided over an era that was the all-time low point in Alabama football history. Whitworth's first season, an 0-10 disaster in 1955, was followed by identical 2-7-1 records in 1956 and 1957. While Whitworth was compiling his unsurpassed record for ineptitude, Bama alumnus Paul (Bear) Bryant was turning Texas A&M into a national power, and this was after he had previously completed successful coaching stints at Kentucky and Maryland. When Bryant accepted the Bama job in 1958, he explained his return to Tuscaloosa by saying that "Mama called."

When Paul Bryant returned to his alma mater, he realized that the talent level in Tuscaloosa was extremely low. He immediately set to work signing a huge recruiting class, and whipping the remnants left by Whitworth into as competitive a team as possible. Bryant's first team would compile only a 5-4-1 record and was his only Alabama team that failed to go to a bowl. His 1959 team improved to 7-2-2, which included a 7-0 Liberty Bowl loss to Penn State. The record improved to 8-1-2 in 1960, and that squad had the nucleus for the first Bryant team to make a run for the national championship.

Bryant had told his 1958 recruiting class that if they bought into his program, they would have a chance to win a national championship by the time they were seniors. True to his word, Alabama was considered a strong contender for national honors as the 1961 season started.

The leader of the team was All-American quarterback Pat Trammell. Although Trammell did not throw perfect spiral passes, he was an accurate passer and had an outstanding football mind. Bama's All-American quarterback did a masterful job of running Bryant's option offense, and he was also an outstanding leader who was as demanding of his teammates as was his hard-boiled head coach.

After his graduation from the university, Trammell became a medical doctor in 1966, but two years later he died after being stricken with testicular cancer. Coach Bryant said that the day Trammell died was the "saddest day of my life," and tears streamed down the coach's cheeks as he escorted the quarterback's mother from the church after Pat's funeral. The church scene after the funeral is believed to be the only time Bryant was seen weeping in public.

The outstanding lineman on the 1961 team was All-American tackle Billy Neighbors, who later became a star in the fledgling American Football League. Junior linebacker Lee Roy Jordan was a ferocious tackler, who Bryant said would tackle any ball carrier who stayed inbounds. As proof of his ability to track down ball carriers, Jordan made thirty-one tackles against Oklahoma in the 1963 Orange Bowl. Junior fullback Mike Fracchia was a quick, hard-nosed runner and the leading Bama rusher in 1961. The heart and soul of the team was a tenacious defense that surrendered a total of twenty-five points in eleven games. The defense shut out six opponents, held two opposing teams to a field goal, and allowed only a single touchdown to the three teams that managed to get into the end zone.

Bama opened the 1961 season with a 32-6 thrashing of Georgia, but they were not as sharp in a 9-0 shutout of Tulane in the second game. After a 35-6 rout of Vanderbilt, the Tide found themselves trailing for the first time that season when North Carolina State took a 7-0 lead midway through the second quarter. However, Bama responded quickly. Trammell threw two touchdown passes to give the Tide a 12-7 halftime lead, and they added two more second-half TD's to end up with a 26-7 triumph. Trammell completed 10 of 14 passes to outshine heralded N.C. State quarterback Roman Gabriel, who would go on to have an outstanding career in the NFL. The Wolfpack's second-quarter touchdown was the third (and last) TD that the defense would surrender that season.

Tennessee was next on the schedule, and the Volunteers were a team that Coach Bryant had struggled to beat throughout his coaching career. While at Kentucky he had managed only a 1-5-2 record against the Big Orange, and he had only one tie and two losses in his first three games coaching the Crimson Tide versus UT. After Tennessee took an early 3-0 lead on a 53-yard field goal, Alabama squelched any talk of a Bryant jinx against the Vols by scoring thirty-four unanswered points. The ferocious Crimson Tide defense held UT to 38 rushing yards and 23 passing yards.

After surrendering the long field goal to Tennessee, the Crimson Tide defense went from spectacular to unbelievable. They shut out their next five opponents to end the regular season with a streak of twenty-three consecutive quarters without allowing a point. At the end of the season, Coach Bryant said that the defense "played like it was a sin to give up a point." The offense did not do badly either as they scored 17 points against Houston, 24 on Mississippi State, 66 versus hapless Richmond, and 34 against archrival Auburn. The Tide rang up 185 points in the last six regular season games while allowing the opposition a single field goal. The only close game down the stretch was a 10-0 victory over Georgia Tech in which the defense

Coach Bryant and his all-time favorite player, Pat Trammell, discuss strategy during the 1961 season. Paul W. Bryant Museum.

held the Ramblin' Wreck to 30 rushing yards and 66 aerial yards. The 34-0 rout of Auburn gave the Crimson Tide their first undefeated season since 1945, and Bama also won the SEC championship.

The undefeated Crimson Tide's reward for their outstanding season was a trip to New Orleans to face the twice-beaten Arkansas Razorbacks in the Sugar Bowl. The Razorbacks, ranked ninth in the Associated Press poll at the end of the season, were co-champions of the Southwest Conference. Arkansas also had an outstanding defense that was tenth-best in the nation, and had given up an average of 177 total yards per game (Bama's defense led the nation with an average of 133 yards allowed per game).

Although Alabama expected a tough game from the Razorbacks, the Tide did well early in the game. In the first quarter, it took Bama only six plays to drive 79 yards, with the big play being a 43-yard jaunt down the sideline by Mike Fracchia to the Hogs' 12. Trammell then faked a pass and ran 12 yards through the left side of the Arkansas line behind outstanding blocking for the game's only touchdown. Tim Davis's PAT kick gave the Tide a 7-0 lead.

The defense came through in the second quarter as George (Butch) Wilson intercepted an Arkansas pass in the second period and returned it 17 yards to the Hogs' 20. However, the Tide offense was unable to progress any further, and Davis kicked a 32-yard field goal with four minutes left in the half to stretch Bama's lead to 10-0. Further scoring opportunities were thwarted by a fumble, penalties, and a missed field goal attempt.

The Razorbacks refused to surrender without a fight, and they kicked a 23-yard field goal in the third period to culminate an 83-yard drive. The three points from the field goal were the first points the Tide defense had given up since Tennessee had kicked its first-quarter field goal on October 21. Late in the game, after a pass interference penalty gave Arkansas the ball on Bama's 40, a potential game-tying touchdown pass barely trickled off the fingertips of the Hogs' All-American halfback Lance (Bambi) Alworth at the Tide goal line. Shortly thereafter, Wilson intercepted his second pass of the game just inches from the Bama end zone to end Arkansas's last hope. After the game Arkansas Coach Frank Broyles praised the Alabama defense, saying, "We knew when we went into the game that we would have trouble grinding out yardage against this team. But we never thought it would be this hard."

The Crimson Tide had been ranked third in the 1961 Associated Press preseason poll, and never sank below fifth during the year. They moved to No. 1 after beating Georgia Tech in late November. The final polls were taken after the regular season ended in 1961, and Alabama was ranked No. 1 in both the Associated Press and United Press International polls. The 1961 national title was the first for the Crimson Tide in the AP poll, which was begun in 1936, and the UPI rankings, which were started in 1950.

7
1964:
The Cardiac Kids

AFTER COACH BRYANT WON his first national championship in 1961, the 1962 team reeled off eight straight victories at the beginning of the season to stretch Bama's winning streak to nineteen and unbeaten streak to twenty-six. However, Alabama lost a heart-breaker to Georgia Tech, 7-6, as a two-point conversion try was thwarted when quarterback Jack Hurlbut was stopped just inches short of the goal line. After the loss to the Yellow Jackets, Bama posted a 38-0 victory over Auburn for its fourth straight shutout victory over the Tigers, and closed out the season with a 17-0 shutout of Oklahoma in the Orange Bowl. The Tide finished fifth in that year's final Associated Press poll.

The 1963 record was only 9-2 with losses to Florida and Auburn providing the two blemishes. The Tide slipped to No. 8 in the 1963 AP poll, but closed the season with a 12-7 upset of the undefeated Ole Miss Rebels in the 1964 Sugar Bowl game. The Sugar Bowl game was played in Tulane Stadium, which was encircled by snow after three inches had fallen in New Orleans on the night before the game.

The 1964 edition of the Crimson Tide was nicknamed "the Cardiac Kids" because of their penchant for last-minute victories in the latter portion of the season. After relatively easy victories in the first five games of the year, Bama twice had to come back from seven-point deficits to beat undefeated Florida. The Gators were led by sophomore quarterback Steve Spurrier, and Alabama's final margin of victory did not come until David Ray kicked a 21-yard field goal with 3:06 left in the game to break a 14-14 tie. After Ray booted the field goal, Spurrier led a last-gasp drive that reached the Bama 7, where the Gators missed a field goal as time expired.

The week after the Florida squeaker, Alabama spotted Mississippi State a 6-0 lead before responding with twenty-three unanswered points to claim a 23-6 victory. Next, a lost Crimson Tide fumble helped LSU to an early 6-0 lead, and, although Bama came back to gain a 7-6 advantage, the Bengal Tigers wasted no time in

Joe Namath (12), whom Coach Bryant called the best athlete he ever coached, and star receiver and future Alabama coach, Ray Perkins (88) celebrate a 1964 touchdown. Paul W. Bryant Museum.

kicking a field goal to give them a 9-7 halftime lead. LSU did not relinquish the lead until Bama's Ray kicked a 36-yard field goal on the first play of the final period.

Although Bama added a touchdown on an interception return, the Tigers' wide-open passing attack twice moved them deep into Tide territory late in the game. One LSU thrust ended when little-used defensive tackle Frankie McClendon batted down three straight passes, and an interception ended the second threat. After the narrow defeat of LSU, the Crimson Tide was locked in a scoreless deadlock with Georgia Tech late in the first half. Quarterback Joe Namath, who had injured his knee earlier in the season, had not started against the Yellow Jackets.

However, with slightly less than two minutes left in the first half, Tide fans roared as Coach Bryant sent Namath into the game after Bama recovered a Tech fumble on the Jacket 49. The future hall of fame quarterback wasted little time as he hit Ray with a pass to the Tech 1-yard line, and on the next play fullback Steve Bowman barreled into the end zone to give Alabama a 7-0 lead.

On the ensuing kickoff the Crimson Tide caught Tech napping and recovered an onside kick on the Yellow Jacket 48. Namath then tossed a 45-yarder to Raymond Ogden, and followed with a 3-yarder to Ray to finish the fourteen-point flurry just before halftime. Bama added ten more second-half points before Tech scored a meaningless touchdown with twenty-one seconds left to close out the 24-7 Tide triumph.

Alabama trailed Auburn 7-6 at the halfway point of their 1964 grudge match, but Raymond Ogden returned the second-half kickoff 107 yards, and Steve

Sloan ran for a two-point conversion to give the Tide a 14-7 lead. Another Tide touchdown early in the fourth quarter was matched by a late, meaningless Auburn score and Bama claimed a 21-14 win.

The victory over LSU had sewn up Alabama's seventh SEC championship, and they played the fifth-ranked and defending national champion Texas Longhorns in the 1965 Orange Bowl. That year's game in Miami was the first time that a bowl game had ever been played on prime time television, and Namath, still hobbled by a knee injury, sat on the bench as Bama spotted the Longhorns an early 14-0 lead. However, Namath replaced Steve Sloan at quarterback in the second quarter and led the Crimson Tide on an 87-yard scoring drive to cut the Texas lead to 14-7. Texas responded with another touchdown late in the quarter to increase their lead to 21-7 at halftime.

Namath, whom Bryant would later call the best athlete he ever coached, gave the national TV audience a lesson in courage in the second half. Most of the gimpy-kneed signal caller's 255 passing yards came in the final half, and they helped cut the Texas lead to 21-17. With about seven minutes left in the final period, the Tide defense forced a fumble by the Longhorns and recovered the ball at the UT 34. Namath promptly led Alabama on a drive that reached the Texas 1-foot line. On fourth down Namath ran a quarterback sneak.

Texas's All-American linebacker Tommy Nobis crashed into the Tide quarterback at the goal line, and the game officials ruled that Namath (who was named the game MVP) had been stopped just short of the goal. Nobis agreed with the game officials' call, of course, but Bama partisans have always favored Namath's version of events in which he said, "All that I know is that when I gave the ball to the official we were both standing in the end zone."

Alabama had been ranked No. 2 behind Notre Dame for most of the season, but when the Irish were beaten 20-17 by USC in the last game of the 1964 season, the Crimson Tide was proclaimed national champions in both the final AP and UPI polls. Both polls were conducted after the regular season ended in 1964, and Alabama's Orange Bowl defeat had no impact upon that year's national title.

8
1965:
Back-to-Back

NO SOONER HAD THE dust settled on the 1964 national championship than Coach Bryant and the coaching staff began preparation for the 1965 season. The most obvious loss from the 1964 champions was quarterback Joe Namath. The departed native of Beaver Falls, Pennsylvania, had signed a contract with the New York Jets for the unheard-of sum of $427,000. The salary seems like chicken feed for today's athletes, but in 1964 baseball superstars Willie Mays and Mickey Mantle sat at the top of the salary range in their sports with annual salaries of $100,000, and paying more than four hundred thousand dollars to a rookie quarterback with a bad knee seemed like a joke. Nineteen sixty-four had also been the last year for Raymond Ogden, one of

Namath's favorite receivers, and All-American offensive linemen Dan Kearley and Wayne Freeman were also lost to graduation.

Although he did not have Namath's proclivity for off-the-field hijinks, Steve Sloan had quarterbacked Alabama to its 1964 Sugar Bowl upset victory over Ole Miss when Namath was suspended for breaking team rules. Sloan had also filled in frequently in 1964 when Namath was sidelined with his bad knee. Sloan also led the Tide to their 1964 victory over Steve Spurrier's undefeated Florida Gators. In 1964 Sloan had been primarily a running quarterback, but his passing ability was utilized more in 1965 as that year's team was blessed with a stable of outstanding receivers including Ray Perkins, Dennis Homan, Wayne Cook, and Tommy Tolleson. Bama's outstanding offensive line was anchored by All-American center Paul Crane and tackle Cecil Dowdy, whom Coach Bryant called one of the finest blocking tackles he had ever coached. All-SEC running back Steve Bowman, the Tide's leading rusher in 1964, also returned for his senior season in 1965.

Despite the usual lofty expectations in Tuscaloosa, the 1965 season got off to a less-than-promising start when Georgia sprang an 18-17 upset in the first game of the season. Although Bama had fallen behind the Bulldogs 10-0 in the second quarter, David Ray had kicked a field goal just before halftime to cut the deficit to 10-3.

The Crimson Tide seemed to be in control when their third-period touchdown tied the score, and another TD in the fourth quarter gave them their first lead of the day 17-10. With two minutes left to play the score was still 17-10, and the Bulldogs, who had the ball on their own 27, seemed to be in dire straits. Georgia decided to resort to a trick hook-and-ladder play in which end Pat Hodgson would catch a pass, and then lateral to halfback Bob Taylor. As the play developed, the throw was a little longer than planned, and Hodgson had to leap to catch it; when he completed the catch he had both of his knees planted firmly on the Sanford Stadium turf before he lateraled to Taylor, who ran into the Tide end zone. However, this was well before the days when controversial plays could be reviewed by officials via video replays, and the game officials let the tainted touchdown stand. Georgia then completed a pass for a two-point conversion and the 18-17 victory that set off a wild celebration in Athens.

After the loss to Georgia the Crimson Tide trounced an over-matched Tulane, 27-0. Next came a classic showdown with Coach Johnny Vaught's Ole Miss Rebels. Ole Miss kicked a field goal in the first quarter, and then scored a touchdown midway through the second period to take a 9-0 lead. However, the

Crimson Tide put together a touchdown drive that culminated in a five-yard run and a Ray PAT kick cut the Ole Miss lead to 9-7 at halftime.

After a scoreless third quarter, Ole Miss added a touchdown early in the fourth quarter to increase their lead to 16-7. Bama immediately responded with a 37-yard field goal by Ray to cut the lead to 16-10, and after the Tide defense held the Rebels, Bama took possession of the ball on their own 11-yard line with 7:33 remaining. Sloan then led Alabama on a methodical fourteen-play drive that ended with a 9-yard TD run by the quarterback, and Ray's PAT kick gave the Tide a 17-16 victory. During the winning drive, Sloan converted three times on crucial fourth-down situations. At that time, the rules allowed a tackle to become an eligible receiver by lining up a step behind the line of scrimmage, and Bama tackle Jerry Duncan used the ploy on one of the key fourth-down conversions. Ole Miss's Vaught complained bitterly about Alabama's use of the trick play and later influenced the rules committee to outlaw it.

After the miraculous escape against Ole Miss, the Crimson Tide traveled to Nashville to play traditional SEC doormat Vanderbilt. The Commodores came into the game ready to play, and Bama seemed to have a letdown after the Ole Miss game. A 69-yard punt return in the second quarter staked Vandy to a 7-0 lead, and the Tide did not score until a 2-yard run by Steve Bowman cut the deficit to 7-6 with only nine minutes left to play. After Bowman's score, Sloan threw a two-point conversion pass to Ray to give Alabama a one-point lead. Shortly thereafter, defensive back John David Reitz gave the Tide some breathing room when he picked off a Vandy pass and returned it 35 yards for a TD. Steve Bowman added another TD on a 57-yard gallop straight up the middle to close out the scoring in a 22-7 game that was a lot closer than the final score indicated.

After Stabler's run, the Legion Field scoreboard erroneously showed it to be third down, and when Stabler saw the scoreboard he threw the ball out of bounds to stop the clock.

The 1965 game against the Tennessee Volunteers was another classic in the "third Saturday in October" series and a source of great frustration for Alabama fans. Although the Vols took a 7-0 lead midway through the second quarter, a 1-yard run by quarterback Sloan tied the game 7-7 with only one second left on the clock before halftime.

From a statistical standpoint, Alabama completely dominated the game as they racked up 361 yards of total offense while holding UT to only 195. However, the Crimson Tide was unable to convert the statistical advantage into a victory on the scoreboard. Late in the game the Tide mounted one last drive to attempt to snatch a victory over their rivals to the north. Kenny Stabler replaced Sloan at quarterback on the last drive, and on third down he raced down close to the UT goal line. After Stabler's run, the Legion Field scoreboard erroneously showed it to be third down, and when Stabler saw the scoreboard he threw the ball out of bounds to stop the clock and set up a game-winning field goal. After the game, Coach Bryant took full responsibility for the faulty last-second communication, but he also pointed out that his team still had a chance to repeat as national champions.

After a decisive 21-0 victory over Florida State, the Mississippi State game proved to be Bama's biggest test in the last part of the season. Although the Tide scored on a 65-yard, Sloan-to-Dennis Homan pass on the first play of the game, and later added a Ray field goal to build the lead to 10-0, the Bulldogs refused to give up. They responded to Ray's field goal with a touchdown to cut the Bama lead to 10-7, and threatened to go ahead several times late in the game. However, despite State's persistence, the Crimson Tide defense made big plays when they had to, to seal the 10-7 victory.

After the Mississippi State thriller, the Tide hit their stride with blowout victories over LSU and South Carolina, and ended the regular season with a 30-3 rout of in-state rival Auburn. The victory over Auburn wrapped up the second consecutive SEC title for Alabama, and Bryant continued to insist his team had a shot at the national title if they could defeat Nebraska in the 1966 Orange Bowl.

The national polls had been criticized for crowning the 1964 national champion after the end of the regular season and prior to the bowl games, and the Associated Press responded in 1965 by delaying the final voting until after the bowl games had been played. The early vote in 1964 had helped Alabama when the Crimson Tide lost their bowl game to Texas, and Coach Bryant saw the late voting as a chance for the Tide to successfully defend its national title despite its 9-1-1 record in the regular season. Although the late voting would give the fourth-ranked Tide the possibility of winning another national title, it was a slim chance at best as they would need plenty of help. First, the No. 1 team, undefeated Michigan State, was a decided favorite over UCLA in the Rose Bowl. The Spartans had defeated the Bruins 13-3 in the season opener, and they were fourteen-point favorites to defeat UCLA in the Pasadena bowl. Next, second-ranked Arkansas carried a twenty-two-game winning streak into its Cotton Bowl date with the 7-3 LSU Tigers (whom Alabama had thumped, 31-7), and the Razorbacks were prohibitive favorites to stretch their winning streak to twenty-three in Dallas. If Arkansas and Michigan State lost their day-time games, it would be up to the Crimson Tide to take care of the other team above them, third-ranked Nebraska, which was their opponent in the prime-time Orange Bowl game.

Coach Bryant had spelled out to his players the scenario that could put his Crimson Tide back on top of the world of college football, and as the bowl games were played on January 1, 1966, his prophecies eerily started to come true. The first highly ranked team to take the field was Arkansas, and the Hogs only took one minute and twenty-seven seconds to cover 87 yards and score a TD to take a 7-0 lead over LSU. However, the unranked Tigers gave up no more points and scored fourteen themselves to knock off the first team standing in Bama's path to a national title. Later that afternoon out on the West Coast, UCLA scored two second-period TD's to take a 14-0 lead over Michigan State. Although the Spartans scored two second-half touchdowns, they failed to convert PAT's after either score and lost, 14-12.

After the Rose Bowl ended with a UCLA victory, the Alabama players started to think that their coach was a prophet, but they realized it would take more than a prophetic vision to get past the third-ranked and undefeated Nebraska Cornhuskers. For starters, the Midwesterners had a huge offensive line that had allowed them to dominate opponents as they averaged 290 rushing yards and thirty-two points per game during the regular season. While the weights of the Alabama linemen ranged from 176 to 204 pounds, the behemoths from Nebraska tipped the scales at between 220 and 270 pounds. Although his line was outweighed by fifty pounds per man, Coach Bryant did a masterful job of preparing the players the week of the game, and the chance to repeat as national champions gave the team even more motivation.

Coach Bryant had made his reputation as a coach who stressed a conservative ball control offense and a stingy defense, but he had no desire to get into a smash-mouth slugfest with the monstrous Cornhuskers. Despite the lack of size, his players used their quickness to outmaneuver the opposition. Additionally, Steve Sloan had developed into an outstanding passer as the 1965 season progressed, and Tolleson, Perkins, and Homan were effective receivers.

As the Tide prepared for the Orange Bowl, Bryant told Sloan to "throw the ball any time you want, on any down, and on any part of the field." The quarterback was so astounded by Bryant's instructions that he asked the coach if he was sure he wanted to play such a wide-open style. Alabama set the tone for the game when they ran a tackle-eligible pass to Jerry Duncan on their first play, and it didn't take them long to cover 61 yards through the air on their first drive and take a 7-0 lead over the surprised Nebraskans. Although the Cornhuskers came back to tie the score early in the second period, Bama then unleashed an aerial assault that led to seventeen second-quarter points and sent the Tide to the locker room at the intermission with a 24-7 lead.

Nebraska scored on a long pass early in the third period, but the missed PAT left them trailing 24-13. By the end of the third period, the Tide had racked up another TD and two-point conversion to increase their lead to 32-13 with only a quarter left to play. The teams then traded fourth-period TD's to give Bama a 39-20 lead before Nebraska scored a meaningless touchdown at the end to bring the final score to 39-28.

Sloan broke the Orange Bowl passing record as he connected on 20 of 29 passes for 276 yards, and Perkins had 10 catches for 159 yards.

Sloan broke the Orange Bowl passing record as he connected on 20 of 29 passes for 276 yards, and Perkins had 10 catches for 159 yards. Nebraska's offense was held to 232 rushing yards, which was almost 60 yards below their average, and the quick Alabama defenders had forced and recovered four fumbles and intercepted one Cornhusker pass as the Crimson Tide pulled off one of the most improbable national championships ever in their illustrious football history.

9
1973:
Back on Top Again

AFTER THE IMPROBABLE 1965 national title, the 1966 team finished a perfect season with a 34-7 thrashing of Nebraska in the Sugar Bowl. The gods who control the national polls did not smile upon the 1966 edition of the Crimson Tide, despite the facts they were the defending national champions and had compiled a perfect record, Michigan State and Notre Dame were consistently ranked ahead of third-ranked Alabama throughout the season, and media darling Notre Dame *won* the national championship when it made no effort to score in the latter part of a 10-10 tie with the Spartans. Detractors of Fighting Irish Coach Ara Parseghian said he had decided to "tie one for the Gipper."

Alabama's 1967 and 1968 teams each would win *only* eight games, and the 1969 and 1970 squads provided the low points of Bryant-coached Bama teams as they could manage only six wins each season. The 1970 team had a high-powered, pass-oriented offense, but a feeble defense gave up 264 points. Before the 1971 season began, Coach Bryant decided to change to the wishbone offense, which featured a methodical rushing attack that would keep his offense on the field longer and thus lessen the pressure on the defense. The change in offenses worked as the Tide scored 368 points in 1971 (34 more than in 1970), but allowed the opposition only 122 points or 142 less than 1970. Alabama, which would win more games in the 1970's than any college team had ever won in a decade, won the SEC championship in both 1971 and 1972, and won twenty-one games in the two years while losing only three. Bama finished fourth in the 1971 poll, and seventh in 1972.

Coach Bryant decided to change to the wishbone offense, which featured a methodical rushing attack that would keep his offense on the field longer and thus lessen the pressure on the defense.

By the time the 1973 season arrived, the Crimson Tide had been running the wishbone offense two years, and their recruiting had produced a team well suited to the option attack. Junior quarterback Gary Rutledge was a fine runner who did an outstanding job of reading defenses and had the knack for quickly deciding whether to keep the football or hand off to his teammates in the backfield. Rutledge's backup, Richard Todd, was an outstanding athlete who was a threat to run or pass. Halfback Wilbur Jackson, the first African American offered a football scholarship at Alabama, had been recruited as a receiver, but after being moved into the backfield during his junior season in 1972, he had averaged 7.1 yards per carry. In addition to Jackson, the backfield was loaded with talented runners, including Randy Billingsley, Paul Spivey, and freshman Calvin Culliver. If defenses became too aggressive at stopping the running game, Wayne Wheeler was an outstanding receiver. The rugged offensive line was led by tackle Buddy Brown. Coach Bryant compared linebacker Woodrow Lowe to all-time great Lee Roy Jordan, and Mike DuBose and Wayne Hall were excellent at backing up the line. Mike Washington, Robin Cary, and Ricky Davis were fine defensive backs, and John Croyle and Randy Hall were solid performers on the defensive line.

Any overconfidence that resulted from the rout of California was soon dispelled in the SEC opener with Kentucky, when the Wildcats took a 14-0 halftime lead.

Although Alabama was not ranked in the top five in the 1973 pre-season polls, the Crimson Tide rose to

No. 4 after a season-opening 66-0 defeat of California. Any over-confidence that resulted from the rout of California was soon dispelled in the SEC opener with Kentucky, when the Wildcats took a 14-0 halftime lead. However, freshman Willie Shelby took the second-half kickoff at the goal line and did not stop running until he had reached the UK end zone, and Bama scored two more third-quarter TD's plus one in the final period to win the conference opener 28-14.

The UK comeback was followed by a 44-0 mauling of Vanderbilt in which the Tide wishbone attack amassed 578 yards of total offense. Georgia provided stiffer resistance than the Commodores, as the Bulldogs held a 14-13 lead with 2:45 left in the game. However, the Crimson Tide came back to score two TD's in the final three minutes to win 28-14. Next came a 35-14 victory over Florida in which the Tide scored two fourth-quarter touchdowns after the Gators had reduced an early 21-point Bama lead to 21-14 in the third period.

When the annual "third Saturday in October" showdown with Tennessee rolled around, the Vols came out ready to shut down the run-oriented wishbone. Although Bama crossed up the UT defense by throwing an 80-yard TD pass on the first play of the game, the Volunteers fought back to tie the game at 21-21 in the third period. However, Robin Cary returned a punt 64 yards for a touchdown to break the tie. Shortly thereafter Wilbur Jackson scampered 80 yards for another TD, and another fourth-quarter drive led to the final TD in a 42-21 victory.

The next week the Tide ran for 748 yards and piled up 833 yards of total offense in a 77-6 thrashing of Virginia Tech. The rushing and total offense yards versus the hapless Hokies still stand as all-time Bama records. Mississippi State provided only token opposition in a 35-0 Bama shutout, and Miami was only slightly more effective in a 43-13 Tide victory. Although LSU provided stiffer resistance in a 21-7 Bama victory in Baton Rouge, archrival Auburn was thumped 35-0 to close out the regular season.

The victory over Florida propelled Alabama to No. 2 in the polls, and they moved into the top spot after they beat LSU while previous front runner Ohio State played Michigan to a 10-10 tie. The Associated Press decided to delay naming the 1973 national champion until after the bowl games, but the UPI crowned Alabama as the national champion after the regular season ended. The Sugar Bowl, which was to be played on New Year's Eve, had a dream matchup between two of college football's most illustrious programs—the Crimson Tide and the Fighting Irish of Notre Dame. Although both had been national powers for decades, they had never met on the gridiron, and ABC hyped the December 31, 1973 showdown to the max. The game lived up to its hype as there were five lead changes and plenty of big plays on both sides, but a missed PAT kick by Bama's Bill Davis proved to be the difference in a 24-23 Irish victory.

10
1978:
The Goal Line Stand

ALABAMA REBOUNDED FROM THE disappointing Sugar Bowl loss to Notre Dame at the end of the 1973 season to post a perfect record in the 1974 regular season. However, the Fighting Irish defeated the Crimson Tide in the Orange Bowl at the end of the 1974 season to spoil yet another season for Bama fans. The loss extended Bama's winless streak in bowls to eight games. The 1974 team was ranked No. 5 in the final AP poll.

The 1975 season got off to an inauspicious start as the underdog Missouri Tigers surprised the Tide with a 20-7 upset victory. Alabama came back to win the remainder of its games. The 13-7 Sugar Bowl victory over Penn State also snapped the program's losing streak in bowl games. Bama, which finished third in the 1975 polls, won the SEC championship for the fifth year in a row to set a record that has never been equaled.

Although 1976 was a rebuilding year, the Crimson Tide still compiled a 9-3 record, which included a Liberty Bowl victory over UCLA. SEC losses to Mississippi and Georgia, however, snapped their string of five consecutive conference championships. The rebuilding effort in 1976 provided experience for a host of talented young players that would prove invaluable to future editions of the Crimson Tide. Quarterback Jeff Rutledge (Gary's brother), halfback Tony Nathan, end Bruce Bolton, defensive lineman Marty Lyons, and linebackers Rickey Gilliland, Rich Wingo and Barry Krauss, and defensive back Murray Legg were 1976 sophomores who would be key components in two outstanding seasons yet to come.

The 1977 team, which regained the SEC championship, had only a single loss to Nebraska to mar the record. When the 1977 regular season ended, Texas sat on top of the national polls with a perfect 11-0 record. Four teams with one loss trailed the Longhorns: Oklahoma, Alabama, Michigan, and Notre Dame. While Texas was losing to Notre Dame in the Cotton Bowl and Arkansas was upsetting Oklahoma in the Orange Bowl, Alabama was pinning a 35-6 defeat on Woody Hayes's ninth-ranked Ohio State Buckeyes.

After the bowl results were in, Crimson Tide fans thought that since the two teams ranked above Bama had lost, the Tide would win the national title. However, media darling Notre Dame leapfrogged everyone to go from fifth place to first and claim the national title. The dream scenario which had materialized to give the 1965 Bama team the national title became a nightmare in 1977.

The dream scenario which had materialized to give the 1965 Bama team the national title became a nightmare in 1977.

However, many of the talented players from the 1977 team returned the next year. The season began with a 20-3 victory over perennial national power Nebraska, and the second game was a 38-20 victory over Missouri in which Bama had to rebound from a 20-17 halftime deficit. Next, the Tide picked up its only loss, a 24-14 defeat by Southern California. Alabama then hammered Vanderbilt, 51-28, before they had a rematch with the team they had beaten to win their first national title fifty-three years earlier, the Washington Huskies. The Tide had to come back from deficits twice before subduing the Huskies in Seattle by a score of 20-17. Although they outgained Florida by 496 yards to 194, they were only able to beat them 23-12 the next week. The "third Saturday in October" produced a 30-17 victory over Tennessee in which the Vols scored two fourth-quarter touchdowns after falling behind 30-3. Next came two games in which the Tide was never threatened: a 35-0 shutout versus Virginia Tech and a 35-14 defeat of Mississippi State. Bama then spotted LSU a 7-0 lead before coming back for a 31-10 triumph. In the Iron Bowl, Auburn led 13-10 in the second quarter before Alabama outscored them 24-3 to win their sixth straight over their in-state rivals by a 34-16 margin.

Alabama had begun the season with the No. 1 ranking in the AP poll, but they slipped to No. 7 behind new No. 1 Oklahoma after the loss to Southern Cal, and Oklahoma remained in the No. 1 slot until they lost to Nebraska in mid-November. After the Sooner loss, undefeated Penn State moved into the No. 1 position, and Alabama moved up to No. 2. Alabama's perfect conference record gave them their second straight SEC championship and earned them a berth in the Sugar Bowl.

In pairing Alabama and Penn State, the Sugar Bowl matchup set up a dream game much like it did with the Alabama-Notre Dame game after the 1973 season. Again, the media hype before the Sugar Bowl was overwhelming. Not only did the New Orleans bowl have the top two teams in a national championship showdown, they also had a match between two coaching icons: Bear Bryant and Penn State's Joe Paterno. If ever a game lived up to the pre-game publicity, the 1979

Sugar Bowl did. Both Paterno and Bryant had built their dynasties on hard-nosed defense and conservative offenses, and the 1979 Sugar Bowl figured to provide an abundance of both. Many Penn State supporters thought that the 1978 Nittany Lion defense was Paterno's best. Although the Lions' defense had been stingy against the run, they had not faced a team that ran the run-oriented wishbone offense that Alabama employed.

Early in the game, the Crimson Tide was able to move the ball, but the Lions' defense stiffened whenever Bama came close to scoring. While the game had been billed as a showdown between the Alabama wishbone and Penn State's defense, the Tide defense also proved to be stingy. The excellent performance by both defenses seemed to portend a scoreless first half. Bama did get to the PSU 22-yard line in the second quarter, but a Jeff Rutledge pass was intercepted and returned to the Tide 37. Penn State was close to field goal range before quarterback Chuck Fusina was sacked to force a punt. After the punt, Bama had the ball on its own 20 with 1:32 left in the half, and the Tide appeared to be content to let the clock run out. However, Paterno saw an opportunity to force a punt and then kick a field goal; the Penn State coach called a timeout. Paterno's strategy backfired when the Tide picked up one first down, and then sprang Tony

Nathan for 30 yards to the Lions' 37. After Nathan picked up 7 more yards, Rutledge threw a 30-yard TD pass to Bruce Bolton who made a diving catch in the end zone to give Bama a 7-0 lead with eight seconds left in the half.

The Crimson Tide mounted another drive in the third quarter, but the usually reliable Alan McElroy missed a field goal. Shortly thereafter, the Nittany Lions intercepted a Rutledge pass on the Bama 48, and Penn State drove for a tying TD with slightly over four minutes left in the third period. Later in the third quarter, Lou Ikner returned a Penn State punt 62 yards down the left sideline to the PSU 11, and it took Bama only three plays to score as Major Ogilvie ran around left end for an 8-yard touchdown. Ogilvie's TD and McElroy's PAT kick closed the scoring with Bama having a 14-7 lead, but that did not end the suspense.

As the fourth quarter commenced, the Alabama defense continued to be as tough as ever, and it was becoming evident that Penn State would need a miracle to have a chance to pull it out. The miracle appeared when Rutledge and Ogilvie messed up an option pitch and the Lions recovered the resulting fumble on the Crimson Tide 19 with 7:57 to play. On the first play after the fumble recovery, fullback Matt Suhey ripped straight up the middle for an 11-yard gain and a first down on the Tide 8.

The next four plays would be forever emblazoned in the memories of Bama fans. First, running back Mike Guman got 2 yards after taking a pitch from Fusina. Then Fusina threw a short pass to flanker Scott Fitzkee, and Murray Legg, the defensive back who was trying to cover Fitzkee, slipped as the receiver ran his pass route. Defensive back Don McNeal was covering another receiver in the back of the end zone, but when McNeal saw Fitzkee break free, he instinctively headed for the receiver. In one move, McNeal seemed to travel from the back of the end zone to tackle Fitzkee a mere yard from the goal line in one of the greatest plays ever recorded in the long and glorious history of Alabama football. On the third-down play, Suhey again tried the middle of the Crimson Tide defensive line, but gained only about eighteen inches.

As Fusina walked back to the huddle, Bama's All-American tackle Marty Lyons told the signal caller, "You better throw."

After the play Fusina came over to see exactly how far the ball was from the goal line, and the quarterback determined that he was only a few inches from paydirt. As Fusina walked back to the huddle, Bama's All-American tackle Marty Lyons told the signal caller, "You better throw." Paterno called a timeout to give him plenty of time to choose just the right play to get the ball into the end zone. After due deliberation, the Penn State coaching icon called basically the same play that he had run on third down, with Guman carrying the ball. As the play developed, Lyons, Byron Braggs, Rich Wingo, and Legg clogged up the line while linebacker Barry Krauss went high to keep Guman from jumping over the line. When the play ended the football was still inches from the Bama end zone. Years later, when Crimson Tide fans hear the term "goal line stand," they immediately think back to the day in January 1979 when their stout defense enabled the Tide to win its tenth national title.

11

1979:

Encore

ALTHOUGH THERE WERE MAJOR losses to graduation from the 1978 national championship team, the 1979 edition of the Crimson Tide was loaded with talent. Alabama started the season in the No. 2 spot in the preseason polls, and never dropped below that position as the season progressed. The team had three All Americans in center Dwight Stephenson, offensive tackle Jim Bunch, and cornerback Don McNeal. An additional eight Tidesmen joined the three All Americans on the all-conference team to give Bama a total of eleven All-SEC players. The all-conference players included linebacker Thomas Boyd, defensive tackle Byron Braggs, offensive guard Mike Brock, defensive tackle David Hannah, safety Jim Bob Harris, defensive end E. J. Junior, halfback Major Ogilvie, and quarterback Steadman Shealy.

The 1979 Crimson Tide lived up to their pre-season hype as they cruised through their first five opponents by a combined count of 219-9. The 30-6 victory over Georgia Tech in the opener was the smallest victory margin as they would go on to crush Baylor (30-0), Vanderbilt (66-3), Wichita State (38-0), and Florida (40-0). After five games, the Tide seemed to be invincible as they prepared for their annual clash with Johnny Majors's Tennessee Volunteers. Majors was in the third year of a rebuilding project in Knoxville, and although the eighteenth-ranked Vols came into the Alabama game with a 4-1 record, their only significant victory had been over Auburn, and they had followed the Auburn victory with a loss to lowly Mississippi State. The Volunteers did not seem to be much of a threat to beat the nation's best football team in its own backyard in Birmingham. However, Tennessee scored a touchdown after recovering a fumble on Bama's 14, and then drove 63 yards through the Crimson Tide defense for another TD to take a 14-0 lead with 1:44 left in the first quarter.

Shortly thereafter, UT drove 53 yards to set up a 45-yard field goal to increase their lead to 17-0 with 12:58 left in the second quarter. Bama came back and scored on a 33-yard pass to cut the deficit to 17-7 before halftime. In the third period an interception of a UT pass at the Volunteer 30 set up a six-play TD drive that cut the deficit to 17-14. On Bama's next possession, a methodical fourteen-play drive culminated in a touchdown to give the Tide their first lead of the day at 21-17. On its first possession of the final period, Bama again took fourteen plays to cover 80 yards en route to scoring the final TD in a 27-17 victory that was the greatest comeback in the illustrious Bama/UT rivalry.

After the comeback win over UT, the Tide reverted to form with a 31-7 victory over Virginia Tech and a 24-7 triumph over Mississippi State. The victory over the Bulldogs gave the Crimson Tide ninety-nine victories for the decade of the 1970's, and a victory in their next game against LSU in Baton Rouge would make them the first team to ever win one hundred games in a decade. To reach the historic milestone, however, they not only had to overcome the Bengal Tigers, but the weather. The game was played in a torrential downpour, and although the Tide had several chances to score, they were unable to put points on the scoreboard until Alan McElroy kicked a 27-yard field goal in the third quarter for all the points needed to give Bama a 3-0 victory. The Tide then completely dominated Miami in a 30-0 shutout before the Iron Bowl showdown with Auburn.

Auburn, which came into the game with an 8-2 record, was led by future NFL running backs Joe Cribbs and James Brooks. After Alabama missed a field goal attempt in the first quarter, Auburn mounted a drive that reached the Bama 12 before the Tide defense stiffened and forced Auburn to kick a 47-yard field goal for a 3-0 Tigers lead just before the end of the first quarter. Bama took the ensuing kickoff and fired up their wishbone offense to march 80 yards for a TD that gave them a 7-3 lead. Auburn then mounted a drive that ended in an unsuccessful 52-yard field goal attempt. After the Auburn miss, Alabama drove the ball 65 yards for their second straight TD to take a 14-3 lead into the locker room at halftime.

After seemingly taking control of the game just before halftime, the Tide developed a bad case of fumbleitis after intermission. First, Auburn recovered a Steadman Shealy bobble on the Bama 21 on the Tide's first possession of the second half. The Tide defense rose up and kept Auburn from scoring and eventually forced the Tigers to punt.

After seemingly taking control of the game just before halftime, the Tide developed a bad case of fumbleitis after intermission.

As soon as Bama got the ball back, Major Ogilvie fumbled and Auburn recovered on the Bama 28; shortly thereafter, the Tigers kicked a 39-yard field goal to cut the Tide lead to 14-6. After the Auburn kickoff, Bama launched a drive that reached the Auburn 16 before Shealy lost another fumble. Two plays later

Cribbs fumbled the ball back to Bama, and McElroy kicked a 23-yard field goal to put Bama ahead and again seemingly in control, 17-6, with slightly over two minutes left in the third quarter.

After Auburn took the ensuing kickoff, the Alabama defense held and forced a punt. However, safety Tommy Wilcox fumbled the punt and Auburn was back in business at the Bama 37. With thirty-seven seconds left in the third period, Auburn caught the Tide defense in a blitz and dumped a 36-yard TD pass over the head of the onrushing defenders to cut the Tide lead to 17-12. After holding Alabama on its next possession, Auburn then drove 67 yards through the air and took an 18-17 lead on an 11-yard TD pass with 11:44 left to play. After the Auburn score, the Crimson Tide players saw their dreams of a national championship flash before their eyes.

Taking possession of the ball after the Auburn kickoff, Shealy engineered a masterful seven-play drive that covered 82 yards to regain the lead. After scoring the final touchdown on an 8-yard run, the Tide quarterback ran into the end zone for a two-point conversion to end the scoring with Bama ahead, 25-18. Although Auburn returned the kickoff to the Bama 31, the Tide defense was able to keep the Tigers off the scoreboard and keep Bama's hopes for a national championship alive.

The victory over Auburn was Bama's twentieth consecutive win, and it also gave them their third consecutive SEC championship (and eighth in the last nine years). The victory also gave the Tide a berth in the Sugar Bowl, where they were matched against Southwest Conference champion Arkansas. The Razorbacks came into the game with a 10-1 record, and they were ranked sixth nationally. Alabama had slipped to No. 2 behind Ohio State in the polls after the close call in the Iron Bowl, and the Tide would need help from Southern California, the Buckeyes' Rose Bowl opponent, if they were to reclaim the top spot.

The Tide got off to a shaky start in the Sugar Bowl as Don McNeal, a hero of the 1979 bowl win over Penn State, set up an Arkansas field goal when he fumbled the opening kickoff. However, the Tide soon drove 82 yards for a first-period TD, which came on a 22-yard run by Sugar Bowl MVP-to-be Major Ogilvie, to take a 7-3 lead, and Bama would never trail again in the game.

Shortly after receiving the kickoff following the Tide's first score, an Arkansas fumble set up a short 22-yard drive by the Crimson Tide to increase their margin to 14-3 before the end of the first stanza. With two minutes left in the first half, Ogilvie returned a punt 50 yards to the Hogs' 30-yard line to set up a 25-yard McElroy field goal that upped the halftime lead to 17-3.

After intermission, Arkansas drove 80 yards for a touchdown, but their failed two-point try left the score at 17-9. Alabama's defense pitched a shutout for the remainder of the game, and a 98-yard, fourth-quarter touchdown drive increased the final victory margin to 24-9. Later that afternoon, Southern Cal knocked off top-ranked Ohio State in the Rose Bowl, and the once-tied Trojans came in second to Alabama in the final 1979 polls. The 1979 national championship was Alabama's eleventh, and the sixth (and final) national title for Coach Paul (Bear) Bryant.

12
1992:
A Defense for the Ages

HEART PROBLEMS LED TO Coach Bear Bryant's retirement after the 1982 season, and he died less than a month after Bama defeated Illinois in that year's Liberty Bowl. Former All-American end Ray Perkins succeeded his mentor as head coach, but his relative lack of success on the field and prickly personality made Perkins less than popular with many Crimson Tide fans. After four years in Tuscaloosa, Perkins took a lucrative salary offer from the Tampa Bay Buccaneers. Perkins's successor, Georgia Tech grad Bill Curry, was never accepted by many members of the Bama nation, and he accepted an offer to coach Kentucky after the 1989 season ended.

The hiring of Curry badly divided Alabama supporters, and after his departure to Kentucky, Athletic

Director Cecil (Hootie) Ingram was determined to hire a coach who could unify the Tide fan base. Ingram's choice to replace Curry and restore Alabama to its rightful place among the nation's college football elite was Gene Stallings, who had played for Bryant at Texas A&M. Stallings had served as an assistant to Bryant for seven years, and he had been on Bryant's staff when the Tide won national championships in 1961 and 1964.

Stallings began his career as the head coach of the Crimson Tide with a modest 7-5 record in 1990. However, after a 35-0 blowout loss to Florida in the second game of the 1991 season, Bama won the last ten games of the season to finish 11-1. Although the strong finish in 1991 had many Crimson Tide fans eagerly anticipating a return to the top of the college football world in 1992, Stallings tried to dampen their enthusiasm by saying that national title talk was premature. When the coach was asked to assess the status of the Alabama program after the 1991 season, he said that he felt good about the Tide's progress, but that they were about two years away from being "where we want to be."

As the 1992 season approached, pigskin experts predicted the Tide would have another outstanding defense along with a mediocre offense. Outstanding defensive players included ends John Copeland and Eric Curry; linebackers Antonio London, Lemanski Hall, Michael Rogers, and Derrick Oden; and defensive backs

Antonio Langham, George Teague, and Chris Donnelly. The offense had an outstanding running back in Derrick Lassic, but the most explosive offensive threat was David Palmer, who was primarily a receiver and kick returner. Palmer was five-foot-nine and weighed only 170 pounds, but he was an elusive runner who had returned three punts for touchdowns in his freshman year. Stallings said, "When Palmer gets the ball, he's hard to get a hold of." Sophomore quarterback Jay Barker was a good athlete, but had only played the position one year in high school and as a replacement for 1991 starter Danny Woodson when Woodson was injured or suspended. Alabama's place kickers had struggled in 1991, and freshman Michael Proctor was expected to provide a quick fix in that area.

In their preseason polls *Sport* magazine and the *New York Times* picked the Tide to win the 1992 national championship, but the voters in the Associated Press preseason poll figured Alabama was no better than the ninth-best team in the country. Alabama had been projected to have a less-than-robust offense, and in June 1992, its main offensive weapon, Palmer, was arrested in Birmingham for driving under the influence. Although the Palmer incident made the cautious Stallings even more pessimistic, senior defensive back George Teague was more sanguine than his coach as he proclaimed on the eve of the first game that 1992 might be a season long remembered in the annals of Crimson Tide football.

Bama's celebration of the Vandy victory was cut short, however, when Palmer was again arrested for DUI on the night of the first triumph.

Although Palmer, "the deuce," was suspended for the opening game versus Vanderbilt for his off-the-field indiscretions, Bama's offense was in large part supplied by "the trey" as Proctor (whose uniform number was 3) kicked four field goals in a 25-8 triumph over Vanderbilt. In an early indication of how the 1992 season would go, the Tide's final touchdown came via linebacker Michael Rogers's 36-yard interception return. Bama's celebration of the Vandy victory was cut short, however, when Palmer was again arrested for DUI on the night of the first triumph. The star's second arrest in three months made Stallings "sick to my stomach," and the coach placed Palmer on indefinite suspension.

In their second game, Bama had to overcome a three-point halftime deficit with a third-quarter field goal and a fourth-quarter TD to subdue a stubborn Southern Mississippi, 17-10. Despite the offensive struggles, the defense continued to shine as it held the Golden Eagles to 28 yards rushing, 26 aerial yards, and three first downs. After the Southern Miss game, *Huntsville Times* sports editor John Pruett said the Crimson Tide defense "may be the best in the nation."

Pruett thought the offense was "average at best," but he thought that it would "be an upset if Alabama loses a game this season." Bama, which had moved up to No. 8 in the AP poll after the Vandy game, slipped back to No. 9 after the Southern Miss squeaker.

The offense, which had been so inept versus Southern Miss, seemed to benefit greatly from a "fire-side chat" with Stallings in the week leading up to the Arkansas game. Derrick Lassic set the tone for the game when he rambled 33 yards for a touchdown on Bama's first play, and the Tide rolled to a 28-0 halftime lead on its way to a 38-11 victory. The final Arkansas touchdown came against the defensive reserves with 1:02 left in the game, and Razorback quarterback Jason Allen called the Crimson Tide defensive line "the best I've seen since I've been here." After the game, interim Arkansas coach Joe Kines presciently said, "We may very well have seen the team that will win the national championship." Bama advanced two slots to No. 7 in the AP poll after the Arkansas triumph.

Apparently Stallings did not have a "fireside chat" with the offense the next week, and their performance against Louisiana Tech was abysmal. After amassing 467 yards against the Razorbacks, they could gain only 167 against a tough Louisiana Tech defense, and the offense could generate only six points on two Proctor field goals. However, Palmer's suspension had been lifted by

Stallings prior to the game, and the scatback weaved 63 yards through Tech defenders on a fourth-quarter punt return to close out the scoring in a 13-0 shutout of the Bulldogs.

Despite the offensive struggles, there were no shortcomings on the defensive side as Bama held LA Tech to 125 passing yards (61 yards came on one pass play) and minus-8 yards rushing. As the 1992 season progressed, Bama followers began to compare the defensive unit to other legendary editions of the Tide, such as the 1961 team that gave up twenty-two points in ten games, and the 1966 team that allowed only thirty-seven. Bill Oliver, who played on the 1961 team and coached the defensive backs in 1992, paid the ultimate compliment when he said that Coach Bryant would have enjoyed watching the 1992 defense. The performance against Louisiana Tech dropped Bama back to No. 9 in the AP poll.

The offensive line gave up five quarterback sacks in the Louisiana Tech game, and Stallings gave them a pep talk prior to the next game against South Carolina. The motivation from the coach seemed to work wonders as the Tide jumped out to a 38-0 halftime lead on its way to a 48-7 thrashing of the Gamecocks. The defense gave up only 191 yards despite playing a large number of reserves in the second half. Bama jumped to No. 6 in the AP poll after the win over South Carolina.

The Crimson Tide struggled the next week to score six points in the first half versus Tulane, but they erupted for thirty-one second-half points to thrash the Green Wave, 37-0. After the offense got untracked, they rolled to a season high 435 yards rushing. Alabama moved up to No. 4 in the AP poll as they began preparations for their toughest game of the season—a showdown with Tennessee. Some of the glitter was knocked off the UT game, however, because the thirteenth-ranked Volunteers had been upset by Arkansas the week before.

The Tennessee game was seen as a showdown between Bama's defense, which was the best in the nation, and an outstanding UT offense led by quarterback Heath Shuler, a dangerous passer and fine runner. Although the Bama defense received most of the pregame hype, the Tide offense made its presence felt as it scored seventeen points in the first half.

Tennessee kicked a field goal late in the second quarter to cut Bama's halftime lead to 17-3, after which Stallings became conservative on offense and dared the Vols to beat his defense. The conservative strategy lost some of its appeal, however, when UT scored a touchdown to cut the Tide lead to 17-10 with 12:53 left to play. The conservative approach seemed even less desirable when UT recovered a fumble by Bama fullback Martin Houston at the Tide 45-yard line with 1:43 to play. That's when the defense came to the rescue. Michael Rogers tipped Shuler's last pass and Chris Donnelly picked it off to insure Bama's victory. Alabama remained No. 4 in the AP poll, and John Pruett proclaimed that the Crimson Tide would be 12-0 after the first-ever SEC championship game, and they would "play somebody big, perhaps Miami, in the Sugar Bowl with the national title at stake."

After seeing Bama rack up 301 rushing yards against UT, Ole Miss decided to crowd the line of scrimmage and force Barker to beat the Rebels through the air. Barker accepted the challenge and completed 25 of 39 passes for 285 yards, as he led the Tide to a 31-10 victory over Mississippi that kept Bama No. 4 in the rankings.

Alabama rose to No. 3 in the polls during the week off after the Ole Miss game, and they jumped on a struggling LSU team the next week. The defense held the Tigers to 22 rushing yards and forced four turnovers in the Tide's 31-11 victory. Bama moved up to No. 2 in the polls after the LSU game when top-ranked Washington was upset. The Tide's next opponent, Mississippi State, had a 6-2 record, but their losses had been to hapless LSU and South Carolina. Bama had just beaten LSU, 31-11, and had not worked up much of a sweat in pounding South Carolina, 48-7, earlier in the season.

The Bulldogs did not seem to be much of a threat, and when Bama rolled to a 17-0 lead with 13:30 left in the first half, the thoughts of Bama fans drifted to the upcoming Iron Bowl confrontation with Auburn. After the Bulldogs cut the lead to 17-3 with a field goal with 5:53 left in the half, Proctor responded with a field goal of his own to give Bama a 20-3 lead as the first half ended.

A seemingly different MSU team came out for the second half, and on Bama's first possession they picked off a Barker pass on the Tide 11. After MSU threw a touchdown pass, another pass completion gave them a two-point conversion to cut the Bama lead to 20-11 with 13:30 left in the third quarter.

When Alabama was unable to move the ball on its next possession, MSU took the ensuing punt and promptly put together an 87-yard touchdown drive through the heart of the previously impenetrable Tide defense. The PAT kick cut the Alabama lead to 20-18 with 9:27 left in the third period. Later in the period, State mounted another drive that culminated in a 27-yard field goal, giving the Bullies an improbable 21-20 lead. The Maroons had outscored Alabama 21-3 since the Tide's early 17-0

> ***The Maroons had outscored Alabama 21-3 since the Tide's early 17-0 lead, and the Tide players saw their national-championship dreams going up in smoke.***

lead, and the Tide players saw their national-championship dreams going up in smoke. Bama had trailed only three times all year, and they had never been behind entering the final quarter.

A weird play allowed the Tide to reclaim the lead early in the fourth period. When a Bama punt was fumbled by MSU's return man, the loose ball was grabbed by another Bulldog who also fumbled, and the Tide recovered on State's 43-yard line. The Crimson Tide then began a drive that reached State's 4, and when the drive stalled, Proctor kicked a 26-yard field goal to give Alabama a two-point lead, 23-21. Shortly thereafter, George Teague picked off an errant State pass at the Bulldog 19, and it only took Bama four plays to get into the end zone to increase their lead to 30-21 and salvage their national championship hopes.

In the regular season finale, Auburn held Bama to a scoreless tie in the first half, but Antonio Langham returned an interception 61 yards early in the second half to give the Tide a 7-0 lead. The Crimson Tide defense held Auburn to 20 rushing yards and 139 total yards in their 17-0 shutout victory over the Tigers, which marked the end of Pat Dye's coaching career.

The expanded SEC had been divided into two divisions prior to the 1992 season. After the expansion, a conference championship game was instituted between the winners of the Eastern and Western divisions, and the second-ranked Crimson Tide represented the West against Spurrier's East champion Florida Gators in the first SEC Championship matchup. The game was billed as a showdown between Florida's modern "fun and gun" offense, and Alabama's old-style, rock-ribbed defense. Florida took a 7-0 lead by driving for a TD on its first possession, but Bama came back to tie the game later in the first quarter. Additional Crimson Tide touchdowns in the second and third quarters gave the Tide a 21-7 lead.

However, the Gators scored a late third-quarter TD, and a poor Bama punt set up Florida's drive to a fourth-quarter touchdown that tied the score, 21-21, with eight minutes left in the game. Like all great teams, Alabama was again in the position of having to find a way to win, and its defense provided the solution. After taking a Tide punt late in the fourth period, the Gators were poised to begin a game-winning drive from their 21-yard line. When QB Shane Matthews tried to throw a short pass on first down, cornerback Antonio Langham hid behind the Florida receiver, picked off the pass, and raced 27 yards to provide the final points in Bama's 28-21 victory. Alabama's victory in the SEC Championship Game clinched a spot in the 1993 Sugar Bowl for the Tide, and the New Orleans bowl arranged a showdown for the national championship when they invited top-ranked Miami to oppose the second-ranked Crimson Tide.

The showdown with the Hurricanes would be a classic match between "old school" and "new school" football programs. Alabama's Bear Bryant had dominated the 1960's and 1970's, winning six national championships with teams that emphasized conservative offenses, hard-nosed defenses, and a strong kicking game. Bryant's teams had been taught to show class, and to let their actions on the field do their talking. The virtues that Bryant taught were evident on the teams of his protégé Gene Stallings. On the other side of the coin, Miami had won four national titles in the eighties and early nineties, and they had favored wide-open passing attacks over the methodical offenses that Bryant's teams had employed. Besides the differences in football philosophy, the 'Canes, first under Jimmy Johnson and now under Dennis Erickson, cultivated an outlaw image and were prone to cocky, flashy behavior. They loved to "talk trash" and taunt the opposition as they strutted around the field after making a good play, and had even been known to sport camouflage as part of their off-field apparel to enhance their bad-boy persona.

Both teams came into the Sugar Bowl as the cream of the crop in college football; Miami had won twenty-nine straight games, and Bama had a twenty-two-game streak. A win over Alabama would give Miami an unprecedented five national titles in nine years, and make them the first team to win consecutive national titles since Bear Bryant's 1978-79 squads.

Miami's passing game featured Heisman Trophy-winning quarterback Gino Torretta and three receivers who had each caught more than forty passes, and it was essential that Bama slow down the aerial circus if they were to have a chance to win. Miami averaged 319 passing yards, while the Bama defense averaged giving up only 139 yards. Miami sportswriter Edwin Pope, in true South Florida fashion, said that Bama's defense had "not faced the combination of brain and arm that Torretta gives Miami." The Tide defense, which Pope found lacking, did have two All-American ends in Eric Curry and John Copeland, All-American defensive backs George Teague and Antonio Langham, and three all-SEC linebackers in Derrick Oden, Antonio London, and Lemanski Hall. In addition to the talented players, assistant coach Bill (Brother) Oliver was known as one of the finest defensive strategists in the game, and he had had almost a month to develop a scheme to thwart the high-powered offense of the 'Canes.

When the game began, it soon became obvious to Torretta that Brother Oliver had devoted more time to devising a defensive game plan than he had spent reading Pope's columns. The Heisman winner faced defensive lines that ranged from seven to eleven players, and he frequently had to call timeout to confer with coaches on the sideline to figure out what to do. Before the game, Miami linebacker Rohan Marley, the son of reggae singer Bob Marley, had announced that Alabama's one-dimensional offense would have no chance against the 'Canes, but as it turned out Alabama was the first team to score.

After Palmer returned a punt 36 yards to the Miami 24, the Tide offense advanced down to the 6 before Miami's defense stiffened and forced a 19-yard Proctor field goal. Although Miami responded quickly with a 49-yard field goal to tie the score at 3-3, Bama scored ten more first half-points before Miami kicked a field goal to end the first half with the Tide holding a 13-6 lead.

The tone for the rest of the game was set quickly in the second half, when Tommy Johnson intercepted Torretta's pass on the first play after intermission. Johnson picked off the pass at Miami's 43-yard line and returned the ball 23 yards. The Tide took only six plays to get the ball into the end zone to increase their lead over favored Miami to 20-6. On Miami's next possession, Alabama put all eleven defenders on the line of scrimmage, and a befuddled Torretta threw a perfect pass ... to Teague. The Tide cornerback sped 31 yards to the Miami end zone to make it 27-6 for Bama.

Teague's touchdown on the interception return gave Alabama fourteen points in sixteen seconds and considerably decreased the strut in the Hurricanes. However, Miami did fight to get back into the game, and later in the third quarter speedy receiver Lamar Thomas appeared to have beaten the Tide secondary for an 89-yard touchdown reception. Thomas had said before the game that he couldn't wait to go up against Bama's "over-rated cornerbacks," but Teague humiliated the boisterous 'Cane when he not only chased Thomas down from behind, but also stole the ball from him. Even though the play was nullified by an offsides penalty on Alabama, it had a detrimental effect on the Hurricanes' collective psyche. While Miami would later score on a punt return, Alabama answered by mounting another drive for a touchdown to make the final score 34-13. Essentially, Teague's thievery on the nullified play had snuffed out Miami's comeback hopes.

Even though the play was nullified by an offsides penalty on Alabama, it had a detrimental effect on the Hurricanes' collective psyche.

Although the Tide's offense had derisively been called one-dimensional by Miami partisans, it gained only 45 fewer yards than Miami's high-octane model was able to amass. However, it was the defense that won the game for the Crimson Tide. The Tide defense held Heisman laureate Torretta to 24 completions in 56 attempts and intercepted three of his passes.

Although Miami players said that Alabama had not played a team of their caliber before the Sugar Bowl, Alabama partisans crowed after the game that Vanderbilt, Southern Mississippi, Louisiana Tech, Tennessee, LSU, Mississippi State, Auburn and Florida had all played better against the Tide than the 'Canes. Alabama had not just defeated the arrogant Hurricanes on the scoreboard, they had humiliated them in front of the entire nation. The tradition-rich Alabama program had fittingly won its twelfth national championship in its 100th year of football.

13
2009:
A New Era

THE SEVENTEEN YEARS BETWEEN the 1992 and 2009 national championships were a tumultuous time in the Alabama football program. Gene Stallings coached four more years after his 1992 championship season, but his successor, Mike DuBose, could only compile a 24-23 record in his four-year tenure; and DuBose's lack of success contributed to his departure.

Next, Dennis Franchione compiled a 17-8 record in two years, but he then decided to make a quick exit to accept a lucrative offer to coach Texas A&M rather than face the consequences of NCAA penalties that resulted from transgressions during the DuBose era. After Franchione's departure, Mike Price served less than six months as coach before being fired when he was implicated in a widely-publicized fiasco with a stripper.

Former Alabama quarterback Mike Shula's 26-24 record in his four years at the helm led to his dismissal, and he was replaced by Nick Saban, who had been a successful college coach at Toledo, Michigan State, and LSU. He had won a national championship at LSU before serving a two-year stint as head coach of the Miami Dolphins. His 6-10 record in his last year with the Dolphins was his only losing record as a head coach, and Alabama Athletic Director Mal Moore convinced Saban that he was the man to lead the Crimson Tide back to its accustomed position among college football's elites.

Saban's 2007 record in his first season was only 7-6 as he worked to rid the Crimson Tide of discipline issues and a weak work ethic that he had inherited from the Shula era. Saban was known as a relentless recruiter, and his diligence in that area produced the nation's No. 1 recruiting class in his first full year in Tuscaloosa in 2008. In addition to the overwhelming success in recruiting, the coach stressed planning, focus, and hard work as the key ingredients in upgrading the performance of the players in a "process" that would improve them as football players and as students, and, most importantly, prepare them for life after football.

The talent infusion from the recruiting class and the implementation of the Saban "process" led to a marked improvement on the field in 2008. The revitalized Crimson Tide went through the twelve-game regular season undefeated and rose to No. 1 in the AP poll in early November. However, the season ended with a loss to eventual national champion Florida in the SEC title game, and that was followed by a loss to underdog Utah in the Sugar Bowl.

Alabama was projected to have a strong team in 2009, but all of the preseason polls had defending champion Florida as the overwhelming favorite to repeat as champion. The Crimson Tide started the season rated as the fifth-best team in the nation, and their first game against seventh-ranked Virginia Tech figured to be a good test of their strength in the new year. Although Alabama scored the first points against Virginia Tech on two first-quarter field goals, poor kickoff coverage (a bugaboo that followed the team from the 2008 season) allowed Tech to return the kickoff after the second field goal 98 yards to give the Hokies a 7-6 lead. Both teams scored 10 points in the remainder of the first half, and the Tide trailed 17-16 at the intermission.

After a scoreless third period, Bama took possession at its own 46-yard line after a punt. On the first play after that exchange, quarterback Greg McElroy hit Marquis Maze with a 46-yard bomb, and one play later the Tide recaptured the lead on a 6-yard run by sophomore running back Mark Ingram. A two-point conversion increased Bama's lead to 24-17 with 12:23 remaining.

Alabama stripped the ball from the Tech return man on the ensuing kickoff, and shortly thereafter Leigh Tiffin kicked a 20-yard field goal to increase the lead to 27-17. It took Virginia Tech slightly more than a minute to score a TD to cut the lead to 27-24, but an 18-yard pass from McElroy to Ingram at the end of a 74-yard drive finished the scoring in a 34-24 Bama victory. McElroy did well in the first start of his collegiate career as he completed 15 of 30 passes for 230 yards. In a portent of things to come, Mark Ingram had a career-high 150 rushing yards on 26 carries. Bama's balanced offense amassed 498 yards while their defense held the Hokies to 155.

Going into the game the two big questions for Bama had been the performance of the new quarterback, McElroy, and the revamped offensive line.

Going into the game the two big questions for Bama had been the performance of the new quarterback, McElroy, and the revamped offensive line. Both settled down and played well in the second half after a spotty performance before intermission. After the game, Virginia Tech's veteran coach Frank Beamer praised Alabama's defense, running backs, quarterback, and kicker Leigh Tiffin. Saban noted, "We made a lot of mistakes, but we responded better to adversity than maybe we ever have."

After having opened against a ranked opponent, the Crimson Tide coasted to easy victories over outmanned Florida International (40-14) and North Texas (53-7). Alabama then opened its SEC schedule against Arkansas and their much heralded quarterback Ryan Mallett. Alabama's highly touted freshman running back Trent Richardson scored the first Tide touchdown on a 52-yard run, and Bama rolled to a 28-7 halftime lead on the way to a 35-7 victory. Mallett, who was sacked three times, faced a ferocious rush all afternoon and completed only 12 of 35 passes for 160 yards while throwing one interception.

Although Alabama jumped out the next week to a 21-6 halftime lead over Kentucky and beat the Wildcats 38-20, the offense never seemed to have the zip it had had in earlier games. However, Ingram, who had gained a total of 197 yards in the three games that followed the season opener, picked up 140 yards against the Wildcats.

Following the victory over Kentucky, the Crimson Tide journeyed to Oxford to play Ole Miss. The Rebels, under then-new coach Houston Nutt, had finished the 2008 season with six straight victories, and were ranked in the top ten in preseason polls. Although Alabama's offense gained 354 yards against Ole Miss, they seemed to bog down close to the goal line, which explains placekicker Leigh Tiffin's five field goals. The only touchdown came when Ingram (who finished with a new personal high of 172 yards) scampered 36 yards after catching the Rebels defense napping just before the end of the first half.

Like his counterpart Mallett at Arkansas, the Rebels' heralded quarterback Jevan Snead faced a strong rush all afternoon. Although he was sacked only one time, Snead was "hurried" all afternoon, and he was able to complete only 11 of 34 passes for 140 yards while throwing four interceptions. The Rebels could garner only 197 yards of offense as they were thrashed by a 22-3 score that was not indicative of how one-sided the game actually was.

After the triumph over Ole Miss, Alabama played South Carolina in Tuscaloosa. The Tide rolled early versus the Gamecocks as Mark Barron intercepted a pass on the first play of the game, and returned it 77 yards to give Bama a 7-0 lead. Tiffin kicked a 25-yard field goal late in the first half to up the lead to 10-0, but the Gamecocks kicked two field goals in the second quarter, while Tiffin was kicking one, to cut Bama's halftime lead to 13-6.

The Tide offense, which gained 356 yards, continued to struggle to get the ball into the end zone. Neither team scored in the third quarter, and about midway of the final stanza Ingram decided to take matters (and the football) into his own hands. When the Tide took possession of the ball on their 32-yard line after a Carolina punt, the hard-charging Ingram lined up behind the center in the "wildcat" formation and promptly picked up 24 yards over right tackle. Ingram then ripped off runs of 4, 5, 9, and 22 yards before ending the drive with a 4-yard scamper into the end zone. Ingram's one-man, 68-yard drive contributed to the 246 total ground yards that he gained to set a new single-game rushing record for Bryant-Denny Stadium. It was that performance against the Gamecocks that elevated Ingram into the race for the 2009 Heisman Trophy.

Following the victory over USC, Tennessee's controversial new coach Lane Kiffin brought his Volunteers to Tuscaloosa for a "third Saturday in October" clash that was actually played on the fourth Saturday in October. Kiffin had made headlines soon after being hired by UT, accusing other SEC coaches, including Florida's Urban Meyer and Nick Saban, of violating NCAA recruiting rules. When it was explained to Kiffin that the opposing coaches had not violated any rules, the head of Vol Nation shrugged it off by saying he was just trying to fire up UT fans. Some observers were left wondering what type of fans were fired up by knowing that their coach did not know what he was talking about. Despite his ability to fire up Vol Nation with inaccurate, wild accusations,

Defensive lineman Terrence Cody blocks a field goal attempt by Tennessee's Daniel Lincoln on the last play of the game to clinch Bama's 12-10 victory over the Volunteers in 2009. AP Images.

Kiffin brought his spotty-performing team into the Alabama game with a 3-3 record.

Against Tennessee, Alabama's offense, *still* continued to have trouble getting the ball into the end zone. The Tide did manage to take a 9-3 halftime lead over the Vols as Tiffin kicked three field goals in the first half while the Bama defense was holding the Vols to a single field goal. The Alabama rushing attack had been moderately successful before intermission, but the Tide inexplicably turned to their sputtering passing game when they got close to the Volunteer goal line. While Bama's inability to score touchdowns would prove to be their Achilles heel, the Vols' kicking game began to emerge as UT's cause for concern when placekicker Daniel Lincoln left a 47-yard field goal attempt short as time expired at the end of the first half.

Although Tennessee dominated the third quarter, neither team was able to score in the period. However, the Vols had started a drive with 2:10 left in the third quarter that would reach the Alabama 26 before stalling. When the drive faltered, Lincoln was called upon to attempt a 43-yard field goal. Lincoln's last attempt at the end of the first half had been short. When he tried to get more distance on his next kick, he kicked a low line drive that Bama's massive defensive lineman Terrence (Mount) Cody jumped up for and slapped back to earth. At six-foot-five and 354 pounds, Cody was the last person you would expect to leap high to block a kick, yet he muscled his way into the Vols' backfield and slapped the pigskin to the turf.

After Cody's block, the Tide took the ball at their own 37 with 10:33 left to play. Bama then gained 31 yards before their drive stalled, and Tiffin kicked a 49-yard field goal to increase their lead to 12-3 with 6:31 left. At that point Bama fans were starting to get comfortable as they knew that Tennessee, which had only kicked one field goal in the first fifty-three and a half minutes, would have to score twice to win the game. After Tiffin's field goal the Tide defense forced a UT punt after only three plays, and it appeared that the game was safely in the win column. However, Ingram fumbled for the first time in his career, and UT recovered the ball on the Tide 43; it took the Vols only eight plays to score the first touchdown of the game to cut the Bama lead to 12-10 with 1:19 to play.

Everyone in the stadium knew that Tennessee would try an onside kick, and the Vols recovered the perfectly executed boot on their own 41-yard line. Now the Bama fans who had been so confident after Tiffin's field goal had given them a nine-point lead were squirming in their seats. UT caused them to squirm some more as they picked up 32 yards to the Tide 27-yard line, at which point Kiffin called a timeout with four seconds left to set up a potentially game-winning field goal by Lincoln. The last-second kick was almost an exact rerun of Lincoln's previous attempt as Cody leaped high and slapped the ball down. When Cody's hands hit the football, pandemonium erupted in Bryant-Denny Stadium at the conclusion of one of the wildest games ever played in the storied Alabama-Tennessee rivalry.

After an off-week for the Tide, LSU came to Tuscaloosa for their annual showdown, which had recently become *the* game to decide the champion of the SEC's Western Division. The LSU rivalry had always been tense as both schools historically had strong teams, but the rivalry had reached new heights after Saban had moved to Tuscaloosa after having spent five years coaching the Bengal Tigers before his brief foray into the NFL. The LSU game had always been a tough, physical affair and the 2009 edition would be no different. Although neither team scored in the first period, LSU started, with 23 seconds left in the quarter, what would be a 91-yard drive that required thirteen plays to generate a touchdown and a 7-0 lead with 9:12 left in the first half.

Javier Arenas returned LSU's kickoff 40 yards to the Bama 49-yard line, and the Tide took eight plays to drive far enough for Tiffin to boot a 28-yard field goal with 5:52 left before intermission. In the third quarter Bama drove 81 yards for a touchdown to give them a 10-7 lead with 11:40 left in the quarter. Although the score came on a 21-yard pass from McElroy to Darius Hanks, Ingram along the way picked up 56 of the yards on rushes and also had a 12-yard pass reception on the drive. Later in the quarter LSU downed a punt on the Bama 1, and shortly thereafter the Tigers scored two points on a safety when McElroy was called for intentional grounding in the end zone. The safety cut the Bama lead to 10-9, and the Tigers later marched 59 yards to a touchdown to take a 15-10 lead with 3:19 left in the quarter. However, LSU's star running back, Charles Scott, broke his collarbone when Bama tackled him after a 34-yard run during the touchdown drive.

In the final period Ingram (who finished the game with 144 rushing yards) again provided most of the offense as he gained 47 of the 64 yards required to set up a 20-yard Tiffin field goal that cut the LSU lead to 15-13. On Bama's next possession, receiver Julio Jones took a short pass and ran 73 yards down the left sideline for a touchdown. Trent Richardson's run for the two-point conversion increased the Tide's lead to 21-15 with 10:24 to go. Later, the Crimson Tide drove 31 yards to set up a 40-yard Tiffin field goal that ended the scoring in the 24-15 Bama triumph. The victory over the Tigers secured Alabama's second straight SEC Western

Division title, and a rematch with Florida in the 2009 SEC Championship Game.

Following the fierce game with LSU, Alabama went to Starkville to play Mississippi State. Although the Bulldogs under first-year coach Dan Mullen were stronger than they had been the previous year, the Crimson Tide offense gained 444 yards while their defense held MSU to 213 yards. The final score of 31-3 was indicative of how non-competitive the game was. Ingram picked up 149 yards on nineteen carries, including one 70-yard dash that would be the Heisman hopeful's longest run of the year. After the thrashing of the Bulldogs, the reserves played a good portion of the game as Alabama ran all over outmanned UT Chattanooga in a 45-0 rout.

As Alabama prepared for the 2009 Iron Bowl, they knew they would be facing a far-superior team to the one they had humiliated 36-0 the previous season. Coach Gene Chizik had replaced the embattled Tommy Tuberville on the Plains, and the rejuvenated Tigers had already qualified for a bowl game. Although Auburn was the Tide's bitter in-state rival, some observers thought Bama was more concerned with the upcoming SEC Championship Game versus Florida that would be played a week after the Auburn game. The fear of Alabama fans that the Tide was looking past Auburn seemed to be borne out when Auburn needed only four

Roy Upchurch hauls in a 4-yard pass from Greg McElroy as Auburn's Neiko Thorpe (15) and Antonio Coleman (52) pursue. After spotting the Tigers a 14-0 lead, Bama worked its way back for a 26-21 victory. AP Images.

plays to cover 80 yards in scoring a touchdown on its first possession of the game. After the quick touchdown, Auburn surprised the Tide with an onside kick which the Tigers recovered on their 42-yard line. The Tigers used a flea-flicker pass completion and assorted razzle-dazzle to cover 58 yards in twelve plays to score another touchdown and increase their lead to 14-0 with 5:42 still left to play in the first quarter.

The heavily favored Tide could see their dream season imploding, but rather than panicking, they set out to stop Auburn's offense and attack the Tigers' defense. Auburn had structured their defense to stop Heisman candidate Ingram's straight-ahead running style, and the Tide countered with freshman Trent Richardson, a more elusive runner than Ingram. McElroy started hitting passes and utilizing slashing runs by Richardson on a 58-yard drive that resulted in a touchdown to cut the Auburn lead to 14-7 with 13:26 left in the first half.

As the Tide offense seemed to show some signs of life, the defense began to throttle the Tigers' spread offense, which apparently had run out of trick plays. With 5:31 left in the first half, the Tide scored a touchdown to tie the game when tight end Colin Peek hauled in a 33-yard pass from McElroy. After Peek's touchdown catch, neither team was able to generate more points before intermission, and the score remained 14-14 at halftime.

On Auburn's second possession of the second half, they caught the Tide pass defense napping for a 72-yard touchdown pass to take a 21-14 lead. Although nervous

Bama partisans could again see the national title slipping away, that was to be Auburn's last score of the day. Midway through the third period, Arenas set up a score when he returned an Auburn punt 55 yards to the Tigers' 33. When Bama's drive stalled at the 10-yard line, Tiffin kicked a 27-yard field goal to cut Auburn's lead to 21-17.

On Auburn's next possession, Mark Barron picked off a pass and returned it 14 yards to the Tigers' 43. The Tide then advanced to Auburn's 14-yard line to set up a 31-yard Tiffin field goal that cut the deficit to 21-20 with twenty-four seconds left in the third period.

After several changes of possession, Bama took control of the ball at their 21 with 8:27 left in the game. Tide fans sensed that it was do-or-die for the Tide's national title aspirations, and the Tidesmen picked the "do" option. It took Bama fifteen plays over seven minutes and three seconds to cover the 79 yards that will always be remembered as THE DRIVE. Using mostly short passes, the Crimson Tide had to convert three third downs as they advanced to the AU 4-yard line, where they faced another crucial third-down situation with a minute and a half left. Following a timeout to set up what could be the most important play of the season, Bama faked a running play and then floated a pass to oft-injured running back Roy Upchurch in the right corner of the end zone. Upchurch's catch gave the Tide its first lead of the game at 26-21 and kept the dream of a national championship alive.

Following the dramatic victory over Auburn, Alabama turned its attention to avenging its loss to Florida in the 2008 SEC Championship Game. Many Tide partisans saw the entire 2009 regular season as nothing more than a prelude to the rematch with the Gators that would give them a chance to restore Bama to its rightful place atop the SEC. However, the Gators had their own opinions about who the premier team in the conference was, and the 2009 Florida team returned almost all of its key players from its 2008 national championship squad. At the top of the Florida talent pool was All American and former Heisman Trophy-winning quarterback Tim Tebow, who carried the nickname of "Superman" through his four years in Gainesville. Besides being an amazingly accurate passer and a bullish runner, Tebow was the inspirational leader of the Gators. Many astute football observers said the Gator QB was simply the best player in the history of college football.

Although Tebow and company were a formidable opponent, the Crimson Tide also had their share of talent; and they were determined to bring the SEC title back to Tuscaloosa. After receiving the opening kickoff, Bama used a spread formation to drive 47 yards to set up a 48-yard Tiffin field goal to take a 3-0 lead with 10:37

left in the opening quarter. The defense then forced a three-and-out on Florida's first possession, and the Tide used a mix of McElroy passes and Ingram rushes to drive 76 yards for a touchdown. Tiffin's missed extra-point attempt left the Bama lead at 9-0 with 5:33 remaining in the first quarter.

Florida took the ensuing kickoff and drove 56 yards to set up a 48-yard field goal that cut Bama's lead to 9-3 at the end of the opening period. Early in the second period, Bama cranked up another drive, this one covering 68 yards, that led to a 34-yard Tiffin field goal that increased the lead to 12-3. Florida responded with a 70-yard TD drive that featured consecutive Tebow runs of 23 and 15 yards, and ended with the QB firing a 23-yard pass into the end zone to cut the Bama lead to 12-10.

The Tide took the ensuing kickoff, and on the first play from scrimmage McElroy threw a short pass to Ingram, and the running back greatly enhanced his Heisman chances when he streaked 69 yards down the right sideline to the Gator 3-yard line. On the next play Ingram scooted around left end and into the end zone to increase Bama's lead to 19-10. Florida responded quickly with a 65-yard drive that set up a 32-yard field goal with just over a minute to play in the first half. The field goal cut the Bama halftime lead to 19-13, but it would be the last points scored by the defending national champions.

When the Tide defense forced the Gators to punt on their first possession of the second half, the Tide offense took only five plays to cover 74 yards. Colin Peek caught a 17 yard pass from McElroy in the end zone to end the drive and increase the lead to 26-13. Halfway through the third period Bama began an 88-yard drive that consumed almost eight minutes, and Ingram capped it with a 1-yard plunge to increase the Tide's lead and set the final score at 32-13. The time-consuming drive erased any doubt as to the identity of the SEC champion, and set up a showdown with Big 12 champion Texas for the national championship. The fact that the 2009 national title game was to be played in Pasadena's Rose Bowl was seen by tradition-conscious Tide fans as a promising omen, since their team would be returning to the setting that had brought Alabama football to the national consciousness some eighty-four years before.

The fact that the 2009 national title game was to be played in Pasadena's Rose Bowl was seen by tradition-conscious Tide fans as a promising omen.

Saban had been successful throughout his career because of his emphasis on hard work, dedication, and staying focused. At the conclusion of the 2009 regular season, players who "bought into" the Saban virtues reaped a treasure trove of individual honors. An unprecedented six members of the Crimson Tide were named All Americans: offensive guard Mike Johnson, running back Mark Ingram, placekicker Leigh Tiffin, linebacker Rolando McClain, nose guard Terrence Cody, and defensive back/kick returner Javier Arenas. McClain, who had led the defense through his three years at the Capstone, won the Dick Butkus Award as the nation's premier linebacker. Although Alabama had a long list of accomplishments on the gridiron, it had never had a player win the Heisman Trophy. After Ingram ran for 246 yards against South Carolina, his name began to appear on the list of Heisman hopefuls that media types obsess over. His performances after the game against the Gamecocks kept him in a prominent position among Heisman candidates until the Auburn game. Auburn stacked its defense to stop Ingram, and his 30 rushing yards against the Tigers on national TV seemed to doom his Heisman chances. However, his performance against Florida's highly regarded defense in the biggest game of the year, the SEC title game, put him back into the Heisman picture. When Ingram ran through the Gators for 113 yards and also picked up another 76 yards on two pass receptions, he earned a trip to New York City for the Heisman presentation. The final voting for the prestigious award gave the Alabama running back his school's first Heisman Trophy.

Alabama's opponent in the 2009 BCS title game, the Texas Longhorns, was one of the few rivals that the

Crimson Tide had never beaten. In eight previous encounters with the 'Horns, the proud Crimson Tide had compiled a less-than-glittering 0-7-1 record. Like Alabama, the Longhorns also went through the 2009 season with an undefeated record, and they were led by a two-time Heisman finalist, quarterback Colt McCoy. Besides the offensive fireworks provided by McCoy and his compatriots, the Longhorns' defense was the third-best in the country in total yardage allowed, and Texas led the nation in rushing defense.

Although Saban is an old-school coach who tries to win with a strong defense and a conservative offense, the Crimson Tide tried to generate some early momentum in the BCS Championship game with a trick play. The Tide offense had lost a total of 13 yards in its first three plays, and Saban called upon punter P.J. Fitzgerald to fake a punt and throw a pass in an attempt to pick up a first down. However, Fitzgerald's pass was woefully underthrown, and Texas intercepted it at the Tide 37. Texas drove to the Bama 1-yard line, where they had a first and goal situation. The Tide defense stiffened with a goal-line stand that forced Texas to settle for a field goal and a 3-0 lead. Even more important than the pass interception on the fake punt, the goal-line stand, or the field goal was what occurred on the fifth play of the game—Texas's All-American quarterback McCoy suffering a shoulder injury on his throwing side that knocked him out of the game. The Longhorns' signal caller had been running an option play around left end when he was hit by defensive lineman Marcell Dareus, and although it didn't seem to be a hard tackle, it caused the quarterback's right arm to become completely numb.

After the Texas field goal, Alabama's special teams made their second serious error of the night when they were unable to field the ball on the ensuing kickoff, and the miscue allowed the Longhorns to recover the ball on the Bama 30-yard line. After the recovery, Texas was unable to move the ball with freshman Garrett Gilbert replacing McCoy, and settled for a 42-yard field goal that made their lead 6-0. The Texas defense stifled Bama's offense for most of the first quarter, but late in the period the Tide resorted to their most reliable offensive tactic—give the ball to Ingram and let him plow straight ahead. After Alabama took the ball at their own 43, they sent the Heisman winner around left end for 8 yards, and then straight ahead for 9 more. After a 23-yard pass from McElroy to Julio Jones, Ingram plowed up the middle for 9 more yards, and two plays later he ran into the end zone to give the Tide a 7-6 lead with 14:18 left in the second period.

Later in the period, freshman Trent Richardson used a devastating block by All American Mike Johnson to romp straight up the middle on a 49-yard touchdown gallop to increase the Bama lead to 14-6 as the Tide started to pick up a head of steam that would take them through to halftime

With 3:50 to go in the first half, a Fitzgerald punt pinned the Longhorns on their own 2. Texas was unable to pick up a first down, and Arenas returned their punt 12 yards to the 'Horns' 29. When the subsequent Bama drive stalled at Texas's 9, Tiffin kicked a 26-yard field goal 29 seconds before intermission to up the lead to 17-6. At that point everyone expected Texas Coach Mack Brown to run out the clock, assuming he would want to hasten to the locker room and use the halftime break to settle down the freshman QB Gilbert, who had played sparingly during the season. However, Brown decided to cross up Bama's defense with a Gilbert shovel pass to running back D.J. Monroe. Brown's gamble quickly turned into a disaster as the Crimson Tide's defensive line surged into the backfield, and when Monroe juggled the ball, Marcell Dareus was again Johnny-on-the-spot as he snatched the ball from the Texan and lumbered his 296 pounds 28 yards into the end zone to give the Tide a 24-6 lead going into halftime.

With the big halftime lead and a struggling opposing quarterback, Alabama's offense went into a shell in the third period. Texas' defense took advantage of Bama's conservative play-calling to completely throttle the Tide's offense in the third stanza. While Texas's defense was stifling Bama's offense, rookie quarterback Gilbert was starting to get more comfortable throwing the ball. Prior to the last drive of the third quarter, Gilbert's passes had gained only 60 yards, but his 44-yard TD pass to Jordan Shipley capped a 59-drive that cut the Bama lead to 24-13 with 1:31 left in the third stanza and changed the complexion of the game.

After the Texas score, Bama utilized Richardson's rushing and a pass interference penalty on the Longhorns to get to the Texas 34. When the drive stalled, Tiffin missed a 52-yard field goal attempt with slightly more than eleven minutes to play. Following Tiffin's missed kick, Gilbert led the Longhorns on a 65-yard touchdown drive that ended in a 28-yard scoring toss to Shipley. The young quarterback picked the Tide secondary apart on the drive as he completed 7 of 8 passes. After the TD, Gilbert completed another pass for a two-point conversion to cut the Tide lead to 24-21 with 6:15 still left to play. What had once been a seemingly safe eighteen-point lead for Bama had shrunk to three points, and again Bama fans were in their familiar squirm mode.

After Texas had crept to within three points of the Tide, Alabama's offense was able to consume only three minutes before punting the ball back to the Horns with 3:14 left. Punter Fitzgerald again came through

Heisman Trophy winner Mark Ingram (22) leads the celebration after defensive lineman Marcell Dareus (57) returned a pass interception 28 yards for a touchdown just before halftime versus Texas in the BCS title game in Pasadena, which Alabama won 37-21. To the left is defensive lineman Terrence Cody (62). AP Images.

with a good kick as he pinned the Longhorns back on their own 7. On the second play after the punt, linebacker Eryk Anders came off the edge and blasted Gilbert on his blind side for Bama's first quarterback sack of the evening. Anders's hit separated Gilbert from the ball, and fellow linebacker Courtney Upshaw recovered the pigskin at the Texas 3-yard line. After the turnover the Texas defense refused to roll over, and it took Ingram's three 1-yard rushes to finally, barely get the ball into the 'Horns' end zone.

The Longhorn defense knew that No. 22 was going to carry the ball on every play, but Ingram was determined not to allow a foot injury that he had sustained in pre-game practice and persistent cramps that had plagued him throughout the game to keep him from getting across the goal line. The running back and the entire Crimson Tide team had pursued the national championship ever since the loss to Florida in the 2008 SEC title game, and they were not going to be deterred from doing what had to be done to sew up the national title. After Ingram's touchdown, Arenas intercepted his second pass of the game at the UT 27 as Texas desperately tried to move down the field. On the first play after the interception Trent Richardson rushed for 17 yards, and a face mask penalty moved the ball to the Texas 5. Two more Richardson runs put the ball into the end zone to increase the final victory margin to 37-21, as Tiffin's final PAT kick was off the mark.

The triumph made Saban the only coach to win national titles with two schools, and he tied Florida's Urban Meyer as the only coach with two BCS championships. Saban joined Wallace Wade, Frank Thomas, Paul Bryant, and Gene Stallings as coaches who led the Crimson Tide to national titles.

A plaza outside Bryant-Denny Stadium contains statues of the coaches who guided Alabama to their previous national crowns. Athletic Director Mal Moore, who had worked tirelessly to bring Saban to Tuscaloosa in 2007, announced after the victory over Texas that a statue of Coach Saban would be added in the future. The 2009 team was the fifth Alabama team to finish national championship seasons in the Rose Bowl Stadium in Pasadena, where the Tide had first captured the attention of the nation eighty-four years before.

APPENDIX
National Championship Sanctioning Bodies

THERE WERE NO UNIVERSALLY recognized sanctioning bodies for national champions in college football until the Associated Press began its poll in 1936. The United Press International poll began in 1950, and the two wire service polls have been considered to be authoritative since they were introduced. A list of sanctioning bodies for Alabama's thirteen national titles is presented below:

1925: Billingsley Report, Boand System, College Football Researchers Association, Helms Athletic Foundation, Houlgate System, Poling System, Sagarin Ratings

1926: Boand System, College Football Researchers Association, Helms Athletic Foundation, Poling System

1930: College Football Researchers Association, Parke H. Davis, Sagarin Ratings

1934: Dunkel System, Houlgate System, Poling System, Williamson System

1941: Houlgate System

1961: Associated Press, United Press International

1964: Associated Press, United Press International

1965: Associated Press

1973: United Press International

1978: Associated Press

1979: Associated Press, United Press International

1992: Associated Press, United Press International

2009: Associated Press, Bowl Championship Series